POLITICAL CONSIDERATIONS UPON REFIN'D POLITICKS,

AND THE

MASTER-STROKES OF STATE,

AS PRACTIS'D BY THE ANCIENTS AND MODERNS

GABRIEL NAUDÉ

1639

TRANSLATED BY

DR. WILLIAM KING, 1711

EDITED WITH INTRODUCTION BY

KIRK WATSON, 2020

Contents

INTRODUCTION

Gabriel Naudé (1600-53), the "politically adventurous librarian" who created the discipline of library science, was also renowned for his writings on politics: his most significant book in this field was *Considérations politiques sur les coups d'état*, which was first printed, in limited numbers, in 1639.

This book is a manual of Machiavellian policy. Naudé writes that "though the Writings of Matchiavel are prohibited, his Doctrine has nevertheless been practis'd by the same Persons, whose Authority has censur'd them". This is an absolutist philosophy of government, based on the idea that the state can rightfully use any effective means to preserve itself from internal threats: its survival will justify any means.

The main tool at the ruler's disposal, *coups d'état*, (translated here as "Master-Strokes of State") is defined by Naudé as: *Bold and extraordinary Actions, which Princes are constrain'd to execute when their Affairs are difficult and almost to be despair'd of, contrary to the common Right, without observing any Order or Form of Justice, but hazarding particular Interest for the good of the Publick*[1].

---

[1] As used by Naudé and contemporaries, coup-d'état referred to action by the state or ruler against an internal faction or segment of its population; it has since taken on nearly the opposite meaning, in which violence is wielded against the

Examples of these *coups* or "master-strokes" are abundant in the historical record, which is precisely where Naudé wishes to put his expertise on display. Ancient and modern rulers, from Moses to Richelieu, have always had recourse to secret, well-planned and successfully executed "stratagems" in support of their rule. These assume nearly any form, from negotiation and decree to propaganda, from massacre to religious charlatanry; the essential features are secrecy, rapidity, and skill in execution: "the Thunderbolt falls before the Noise of it is heard in the Skies...the Execution precedes the Sentence; he receives the Blow that thinks he himself is giving it; he suffers who never expected it, and he dies that look'd upon himself to be the most secure; all is done in the Night and Obscurity, amongst Storms and Confusion".

In his eyes, this is completely natural and right, given the nature of the masses: although himself of modest origins, Naudé had nothing but contempt for the common people: "whatever it thinks is nothing but Vanity, all that is says is False and Absurd, what it dislikes is Good, what it practises is Evil, what it praises is Infamous, and all that it undertakes is pure Folly." The well-ordered government, therefore, should operate in secrecy, removed from public scrutiny: "the People ought to admire the happy effects of

---

state or ruler by an internal party hoping to take over its direction. See Bartelson, Jens. "Making exceptions: some remarks on the concept of coup d'etat and its history" *Political Theory*, June, 1997, Vol.25(3), p.323(24) (https://www.jstor.org/stable/191983?seq=1)

these master strokes of Policy, though wholly ignorant of those Causes from whence they result."

Much of the book constitutes a catalog of these *coups*, illustrating both successes and failures. Among the latter Naudé includes the Saint Bartholomew's day massacre; he calls it "a very just and very remarkable Action", since nothing could be better for France than "the total Ruin of the Protestants"; however, it was botched because its executors were too merciful, too restrained: "It is not sufficient to set out well, but the Course is to be continued, the Reward is at the Goal, and the End regulates the Beginning".

The above passage, and similar sentiments expressed in this book, are probably the reason why Naudé was largely disregarded by Enlightenment-era authors. However, without approving his political views, Naudé's book deserves the attention for the light it shines on the relationship between state and individual in the superintendence of opinion: he is amazingly clear in showing how the powerful instrumentalize ideology and religion to "seduce and deceive the populace".

In this view, the government has a strong interest in regulating philosophy. Beliefs like determinism, atheism, egalitarianism undermine the established order; the state must oversee to ensure that the masses believe:

> That things do not happen by chance or necessity;
> That there is a God that is the first Cause of all

things, who has made a Heaven for the Reward of the Just, and eternal Torments for the Punishment of the Wicked; That some ought to command, and others to obey...That he has a right to levy Money from his Subjects...

For a book dedicated unironically to a Cardinal, this book is one of the harshest and most clear-sighted ever written on the State's use and abuse of religion. Over two centuries before Marx and his opium metaphor, Naudé had already written that: "...it is natural to most Princes to...use [Religion] as a Drug" to uphold their regime. He discusses the false miracles typically used to support the founding of a new regime. He writes that Protestantism exists only because of political reasons.

The book also presents a secularized model of individual conduct and belief, when in the last two chapters Naudé presents the ideal mindset and behavior of the statesman and his advisor: they should accept that the world and its governments are mutable, and that the prince's court is the most fickle of all social scenes. They should be above any superstitious religion: "There is no Occasion for much Mystery and Ceremony to be a good Man".

Thus, the book is also remarkable because of its publication in an age when men could be burned alive for writing against the grain of orthodoxy. On the other hand, several factors sheltered Naudé: his elevated and protected status, the book's secret and limited publication, and perhaps also his grasp of the techniques of "writing between the lines"[2]. In later centuries, this book was inevitably mined and quoted by radical anti-religious thinkers of the early Enlightenment, such as the "Treatise of the Three Impostors"[3].

The translation presented here is as faithful to the original as one could ask for; unlike contemporary translations of similar authors (for example, those of Pierre Charron's *De la Sagesse*), there is no softening of language or any exculpatory notes. It was made by Dr. William King (1663-1712), a lawyer and author of poetry and prose. He was granted a chapter in Samuel Johnson's *Lives of the Poets* (1779-81). Published the year before King's death, this translation was apparently made "to extol the earl of Oxford as a consummate politician"[4].

---

[2] See Leo Strauss, "Persecution and the Art of Writing", *Social Research*, 8:4, Nov. 1941.

[3] See Jonathan Israel, *Radical Enlightenment* (2002), p. 696-98.

[4] *The Original Works of William King, LL.D.*, 1776 (p. xxii-xxiii).

POLITICAL CONSIDERATIONS UPON REFIN'D POLITICKS, AND THE MASTER-STROKES OF STATE, AS PRACTIS'D BY THE ANCIENTS AND MODERNS

Written by GABRIEL NAUDÉ, and inscrib'd to the Cardinal *Bagni.*

= = = = = = = =

Translated into *English* by Dr. KING.

= = = = = = = =

LONDON,

Printed for H. CLEMENTS, at the *Half-Moon* in St. *Paul's Church-Yard.* 1711

To the most Noble PRINCE,

HENRY,

Duke of *Beaufort,*

Marquis and Earl of *Worcester,* Earl of *Glamorgan,* Baron Herbert, and Lord of *Chepstow, Ragland* and *Gower,* Lord-Lieutenant of the County of *Southampton,* Lord Warden of the New Forest, and One of her MAJESTY'S most Honourable Privy-Council, *&c.*

May it please your GRACE,

THE Subject of the following Papers makes it seem proper, that they should be presented to your Grace; for since you have been admitted to Her MAJESTY'S Council, it is convenient you should see all the Measures that have been taken by Persons advanc'd to the like Station. Mr. Gabriel Naude, who was the Author of the French, from which this is a Translation, is accounted one of the most Celebrated Genius's of the latter Age, for his Knowledge of Men and Books, the Variety and Extensiveness of his Conversation, and his good Fortune in being admitted to the Service of the most illustrious Persons then in Europe. His Wisdom, Prudence, good Humour and Temperance recommend him so far, that having studied Physick in Padua, with the famous Mr. Patin, under Mr. Moreau, and being return'd from his Travels, he was in the Year 1630, being then about Thirty, sent by

Cardinal Richelieu *upon an especial Occasion to* Rome, *where he remain'd above twelve Years as Library Keeper to the Cardinal* de Bagni, *a Person that had improv'd himself so far in all good Authors relating to Politicks, and especially in* Aristotle's *Rhetorick, which was his Favourite, that Cardinal* Pamphilio, *who afterwards succeeded by the Name of* Innocent *the Tenth, said he fear'd no other Rival besides him for the Popedom; but Death prevented it. Mr.* Naude *was afterwards Library Keeper to* Antonio Barbarini *Nephew to Pope* Urban *VIII. Upon his coming back from* Rome *he was admitted into the Service of the Cardinal* Mazarine, *of whose Penetration into Mankind the whole World is sensible. To these Patrons he owed his Preferments of Canon of* Verdun *and Prior of* Artige *in the* Limoisin. *Queen* Christina, *who resolv'd to make* Sweden *famous by her Encouragement of Learning, invited him to* Stockholm, *where she shew'd him particular Marks of her Esteem. Upon his Journey thence he died at* Abbeville *in the Year 1653, and so hindred us from several things he had design'd to perfect. Pardon this short Account of the Author, for it is in some Measure an Apology for the Presumption of the Dedication; for I would have nothing approach your Grace, but what had formerly been so far receiv'd in the World as that it might justifie its appearance once again in Publick.*

The Author in this Work has made a sufficient Apology for his searching so far into the Secrets of State, *and shew'd that a great Spirit can have no Prejudice, but rather reap Advantage from the discovery of them. Now if Youth under all the Temptations of the World, can produce commendable Actions fitting the Dignity of a Person's Birth and Grandeur;*

If the strictest Rules of Oeconomy are preserv'd, and Temperance mix'd with the sweetest Affability be always the Product of his Conversation, either in Friendship or Conjugal Affection, the nicest Trials of Humanity, what may be expected from the finish'd ears of such a One, when he knows the Rocks and Quick-Sands he is to avoid, and has no other Port in view but where his Ancestors safely harbored. It cannot be doubted therefore but the Virtues and Honour inherent in your Grace's Family and Person, will always conduct you through the Difficulties of State Affairs, and guard you against the Crafts of Policy, preserving you in the Love of your Countrymen and the Favour of your Prince.

That your Grace will accept of this first Essay of my Gratitude, is the utmost Ambition of

Your Grace's most oblig'd,

Most dutiful humble Servant

WILLIAM KING.

PREFACE of the PUBLISHER TO THE READER.

THIS Book having been wrote only for the Satisfaction of a particular Person, there were but twelve Copies printed, which never appear'd but in some few Closets, where they always held the first Rank amongst such Pieces as were curious: But Chance having given me a Copy, I thought I should not a little oblige the Publick, by presenting them with a Treasure, which before had lain in the Hands of very few Persons. This, join'd to the Merit of the Author, and that of the Work, both which were wrong'd, by not being known, oblig'd me to put it to the Press, and to add the Translations of the Greek, Latin, and Italian Quotations, that are in the Body of the Book, that so more People might be capable of understanding the worth of it; and that it might have that Perfection, which seem'd only to be wanting to it: They who read, will admire this Treatise, and cannot but be pleas'd to have so rare a Piece imparted to them.

PREFACE OF THE AUTHOR.

THIS Book was not composed to please all the World; if the Author had had that Design, he would not have wrote in the Style of *Montagne* and *Charon*, whom he knows to be disagreeable to several Persons, by reason of the great number of Latin Quotations. But as he set about it, only out of Obedience to his Master, he was obliged to keep to the same Discourses, and relate the same Authorities, which he made use of in speaking to his *Eminency*. So likewise it is not to render this Tract publick, that he has put it to the Press, which was set to work, only at the Command, and for the Satisfaction of that great Prelate, who cannot read any thing with Pleasure, unless it be printed; and for this Reason would have twelve Books printed off, instead of so many Manuscript Copies, which should have been distributed. I know very well, that this Number is too small to let the Book be perused by as many Persons as *Balzac's Prince*, and *Silhon's Minister.* But as the Things it treats are so much more important, so it is likewise necessary they should be the less common. In a Word, the Author had no other Design, but the Satisfaction of his *Eminency*, both in the Composition and Publication of these Papers.

TO MY LORD, The Most Eminent Cardinal *De BAGNI*,

My Best, and Most Honoured MASTER,

Non equidem hoc studeo, pullatis ut mihi nugis
Pagina turgescat dare pondus idonea fumo:
Secreti loquimur, tibi nunc, hortante Camœna,
Excutienda damus præcordia.   (Pers. Sat. 5)

'Tis not indeed my Talent to engage
In lofty Trifles, or to swell my Page
With Wind and Noise, but freely to impart,
As to a Friend, the Secrets of my Heart.   Mr. *Dryden.*

MY LORD,

Since You are now at Rome, *enjoying those Honours, which are the Recompence of your Merits, and living in that Repose, which you have happily acquir'd by Your Publick Administrations of seven Governments, one Vice-legateship, and two Nunciatures, I thought I could not better employ that Leisure which your Goodness, and extraordinary Bounty have made me likewise a Partaker of, than by entertaining you with those refin'd Maxims of Policy, and those great Affairs of State, by the Conduct of which, Your Excellency has made your Prudence so remarkable, that the great Genius's who govern all Europe at present, remain astonish'd at it, and have never succeeded better in their most difficult Deliberations and Enterprizes, than when they have been managed by the happy Advice that You have been pleased to give them. For,*

> *'Tis without Fear we cut the foaming Tide,*
> *When* Teucer *bids us go, and* Teucer *is our Guide.*
> Nil desperandum Teucro duce, & auspice Teucro.

CONSIDERATIONS UPON REFIN'D POLITICS, &c.

CHAP. I. *Objections that may be made against this Discourse, with their necessary Answers.*

I Had no sooner, *with much Application*, drawn the first Lines of this Discourse, but that I found my self encompass'd with two powerful Difficulties sufficient, in my Opinion, to have hindred any other Person, that had less Courage and Affection to the work than my self, from going any farther, and to have chill'd the warmest Blood and vigorous Spirit in the pursuit of these Resolutions which may appear no less dangerous than extraordinary. For if the Judicious Poet *Horace* (*Ode* 2. *Book* 2.) could ingeniously tell his Friend *Pollio*, who was going to write the History of the Civil Wars that happen'd in his time.

> *Periculosæ plenum opus aleæ*
> *Tractas, & incedis per ignes*
> *Suppositos cineri doloso:*

The Work to which you now aspire,
Is full of doubtful chance,

Through a vast Plain you must advance,
Where treacherous Cinders hide the Lurking Fire.

What good Success can be expected from any Enterprise that is much more rash and difficult; for not to speak of the Danger there is in trying to penetrate into the Actions of Princes, and to lay that open and naked to View, which they always endeavour to conceal by a thousand Artifices, there are still two others of no less consequence, one of which, as I conceive, may regard and touch your Person, as I find the other will concern my own.

As to the first, I shall freely say, with that Poet who has treated of Philosophy in such beautiful Verse: that he is now the single Maintainer of his Sect:

> *Illud in his rebus vereor, ne forte rearis*
> *Impia te rationis inire elementa, viamq;*
> *Indugredi sceleris.*   (Lucretius *Book* I.)
> Mr. *Creech*.

At least, I in reason ought to fear, that I should wound the Ears or offend the Eyes of your Eminency, and disturb the Sweetness and Goodness of your Nature as well as the Quiet and Integrity of your Mind, by the Recital of so many Deceits, Tricks, Violences, and other the like unjust and tyrannical Actions, (as they must appear at first) which I must hereafter relate, explain, and defend.

If *Æneas,* one of the most resolute Commanders amongst the Ancients, was so mov'd with Pity at the Recital only of the sacking and Ruines of *Troy*, which he made to the Queen of *Carthage*, that he began it with these Words,

> *Quanquam animus meminisle horret Luciuq., refugit.*
> Virgil Æn. 2

> Great Queen, what you command me to relate,
> Renews the sad Remembrance of our Fate.
> Mr. *Dryden*.

And if an Emperor who nevertheless could not escape the Name of *Cruel*, said one day to a Magistrate, who brought a Sentence to sign, by which two poor Wretches were to be condemned: *Utinam nescirem Literas*; I wish I knew not how to write. (*Seneca* Book 2, of Clemency.) May not you have much more reason to wish you had never seen this Discourse, since it entertains you with nothing but what is disagreeable to your Candour and good Nature; should not I do much better to follow the Advice of *Solomon*, *Coram Rege tuo noli videri sapiens*, Don't seem to be wise in the Presence of your Prince; and persue those Studies in which I have been conversant from my Youth, rather than appear before you with these extravagant Notions, as *Diognotus* did with his before *Alexander*; that he might look on him as a great Engineer and Architect. May I not apprehend that I shall have the same Success that *Phormio* the Grammarian had with his Oration, concerning the Art of War, spoke before *Hannibal*, who was esteemed the greatest General of his Age.

And, in truth, when I consider how ill I am provided with means to accomplish so great an Undertaking, which is another difficulty: I have almost a mind to proceed no farther but to quit it entirely.

Shall I that am but a Novice in these Exercises seem so bold as to intrude into Mysteries which are more conceal'd than those of the *Eleusinian* Goddess, without being first initiated; with what assurance can I presume to penetrate into the Cabinets of the Great, and advance even to that Sanctuary where they form their bold Designs, without having had the Address and Conversation of those who manage them? I could not sure be angry with any Person who seeing me persist in this resolution should judge that this was to put a Violence upon Nature which never passes so suddenly from one extreme to the other; or to speak more moderately of it, that there was more Boldness than Reason in endeavouring to sail upon the wide Seas without a Compass, or in engaging my self in a Labyrinth of Subtilties and refin'd Politicks, without having in my Hand that Thread of Knowledge, which might extricate me thence with the Success of a favourable Issue. For it is not here as with those Persons who look upon the Sun with the less difficulty, the farther they are from him; or with Painters amongst whom the shortest sighted make the best Pictures: But rather this Political Prudence is like to *Proteus*, of whom 'tis impossible to have any certain Knowledge, 'till after having descended *in secreta senis*, into the old Man's Secrets, and having with a fix'd and piercing Eye contemplated all his Diversity of Figures, Motions, and Metamorphoses, by which,

—Fit subito sus horridus, Atraque Tigris
Squamosusq., Draco & fulva cervice Leana.
(Virg. Georgicks *Book* 4.)

He not unmindful of his usual Art
First in dissembled Fire attempts to part,
Then roaring Beasts and running Streams he tries,
And wearies all his Miracles of Lies.
Mr. *Dryden*.

However as the young *Aristeus* was not deterr'd by the many difficulties that *Arethusa* set before him from undertaking his Voyage, and thence obtaining afterwards an entire Satisfaction; so these which I have recounted and a thousand others could not hinder me, but that, after I had taken the Councel given by *Pliny* the younger, *Tutius per plana, sed humilius & depressius iter; frequentior Currentibus quam reptantibus lapsus; sed & his non labentibus nulla laus, illis nonnulla laus etiamsi labantur,* The way indeed is safest through the plain, but then it is more humble and depress'd; they who run, fall oftener than they who creep; but then those latter have no Praise though they do not fall, whereas the others though they chance to trip have still some Commendation. I was resolved to set forward in the full Carier of the Design which I proposed.

In answer therefore to the two Difficulties that I rais'd to my self, and, in the first place to that which regards your Eminency, it is not to be mistrusted that these Doctrines do in the least blemish your Piety, or any ways disturb the Quiet and Integrity of your Mind, as at the first blush they might seem to do, and as the three Verses of *Lucretius* would intimate: The Sun displays his Beams upon the most vile and abject Things, and yet is neither blacken'd or defil'd.

> *Nec quia forte lutum radiis ferit, est ideo ipse*
> *Fœdus, non sordet lumen quum sordida Tangit.*
> (Palingenius in Scorpi.)

Though the Sun's Rays strike on the Mud, yet he
Is pure, with Light from all such Mixture free.

The Divines are not less devout for knowing what is Heresy; nor Physicians less skilful for understanding the Force and Compositions of all Poysons. The Habits of the Understanding are distinguish'd from those of the Will: The first appertain to the Sciences, and are always commendable: The second regard moral Actions, and may be either Good or Evil. *Trithemius* and *Pererius* have shewn that it was expedient that there should be Magicians, and that the way should be known how to raise Spirits, that by such Apparitions they might convince the Incredulity of Atheists: Soldiers go often to their Exercise to learn how to trail the Pike, or handle the Musquet, that so they may with more Art and Industry kill Men and destroy their own Likeness: But however they make no other use of them but against the Enemies of their Prince and Country. The best Surgeons study nothing more than how to cut off an Arm or a Leg with dexterity; but it is for the preservation of those who are diseas'd.

> *Truncantur & Artus*
> *Us liceat reliquis securum degere Membris.*
> (Claud. 2. In Eutrop.)

> We thus cut off one Limb
> That so the rest may live in Ease secure.

Why then should a great Politician be prohibited to know when to Exalt or Debase, Release or Imprison, Condemn or Acquit, Reprieve or Execute those Persons he shall think proper to be so us'd for the repose of the State.

Several are of Opinion that a Prince who is prudent and well advis'd, ought not only to command according to Law, but may command even the Laws themselves if Necessity requires it. To preserve Justice in greater Matters, says *Charon*, it is expedient sometimes to relinquish it in less, and it is permitted to do Wrong in the Particular, provided that Right be done in the Main.

If it be objected that it is not proper however to discover such things, and that to Teach them is, truly speaking, to place *Gladium ancipitem in Manu Stulti*, To put a Sword in the Hand of a Fool. I shall answer, that ill People may abuse every thing that is good in the World. Hereticks would ground their Impieties upon the Holy Scriptures. The *Paracelsians* pervert the Text of *Hippocrates*, to establish their visionary Imaginations. Advocates cite the Code and the Pandects in defence of the greatest Criminals, and yet it never entered into Peoples Heads to suppress all these Books. The Sword may as well offend as defend; Wine as well make drunk as refresh; Medicines as well kill as cure; and yet no body hitherto has said that the use of all these is not very necessary. By the common Law of Nature all things are instituted to a good End, but there are Persons who very often abuse them. Nature does not produce Things venomous, that they might serve for Poisons and destroy Mankind, because in so doing she would be destructive to her self: But it is our Wickedness that converts them to that purpose; *Terra quidem nobis malorum Remedium genuit, nos illud Vitæ fecimus Venenam,* Plin. lib. 18. c. I. *The Earth has brought us forth Remedies for all Diseases, and we have turn'd them into Poisons.* But we must go on and say, that the Depravity of Mankind is so great, and the Means they make use of to obtain their designs so daring and hazardous, that to speak of the following *Politicks* as practised now adays, without mentioning these *Refinements,* is indeed to be ignorant of the proper Methods of Instruction which *Aristotle* says are so essential, *Est enim pædia inscitia, nescire quorum oporteat quærere Demonstrationem, quorum vero non oporteat,* It is the Ignorance of Erudition, not to know for what we ought and for what we ought not to seek a Demonstration. Wherefore *Lipsius* and *Charron,* though they were far from being *Timons* and *Manhaters*, yet treated of this part of Politicks, lest their Works should have been imperfect. And the same *Aristotle* who never did anything uncorrect, when he wrote of Politicks and those Governments which were opposite to Monarchy,

Aristocracy, and Democracy, which are Tyranny, Oligarchy and Ochlocracy, gives Precepts for the Faulty as well as the Legitimate. And in this he has been follow'd by St. *Thomas Aquinas* in his Commentaries; where having discommended Tyrannick Government, and dissuaded Persons from it by all the Reasons he could think of, yet nevertheless lays down Rules for the establishing of it, in case any one would be so wicked as to attempt it. And lest this should be doubted, here are his own Words to this purpose, in the Commentary upon the Fifth of the Politicks, Text the XIth, *To preserve a Tyranny it is necessary to kill such Persons as excel in Power or Riches, because they by means of their Authority may be able to rise against the Tyrant.*

"It is expedient likewise, that the most prudent Persons should be dispatch'd lest they by their Wisdom should find a way to expel the Tyranny. Nor should Schools or other Societies where Prudence may be gain'd, be in any manner permitted; for wise Men have Inclinations to great Actions, and are therefore Magnanimous, and easily inclin'd to Insurrections. To maintain a Tyranny, the Tyrant should take Care that his Subjects, should accuse one another of Crimes and Treasons, so as to be in a perpetual Disturbance amongst themselves, that Friend may be against Friend; the Commonalty may dissent from the Rich, and the Rich from the Commonalty; for so they will be less able to do any thing against the Tyrant. Great Tributes and heavy Exactions are to be laid upon the People, that so they may be impoverish'd. The Tyrant should encourage Civil Wars amongst his own Subjects, if he has none with Foreigners, for that will keep them from practising against him. A Kingdom indeed is supported by Friends, but a Tyranny should have no regard to them.

And in the following Text, which is the Twelfth, see how he teaches Hypocrisy and Simulation.

A Tyrant to secure his Tyranny, should not appear Severe or Cruel to his Subjects; for if he seems Cruel he will render himself odious, and so excite them against him; but he ought to make himself rever'd by them, for the Excellence of some eminent Goodness; for Reverence is due to that, and if he be not endow'd with it, he ought to dissemble so as to seem to have it. A Tyrant ought so to behave himself that he may seem to his Subjects to excel in some eminent Goodness, wherein they are deficient, for that will create him Reverence. If he is not possest of the Virtues in reality, yet at least let him make them think that he has them.

These are surely very strange Doctrines from the Mouth of a Saint, and are nothing different from those of *Machiavel* and *Cardan*, and yet may be solv'd by these two Reasons which are probable and right enough. The first is, That these Maxims being so declar'd and publish'd, the Subjects may easily know when the Carriage of their Prince tends to a Tyrannick Power, and so provide for themselves accordingly, as Mariners when they foresee a Storm make the best of their way to avoid it. The second, That when a Tyrant acting without Counsel and Advice would establish his Dominion,

> *Cuncta ferit dum cunta timet grassatur in omnes*
> *Ut se posse putent.*
> > Claudian.

> He strikes at all, whist all he Fears, and Raves
> To make them think that all must be his Slaves.

And resembles a Wolf, who being got into a Fold, tho' he might appease his Hunger and glut himself with one Sheep, yet worries all the rest. But on the contrary, if he proceeds with Judgment and follows the Precepts of them who are better advis'd and less passionate than himself, he will perhaps like *Tarquin* rest content with striking off the Heads of the highest Poppies, or crushing those Spirits which appear above others, after the Example of *Thrasybulus* and *Periander*; and so the Evil that could not be avoided will become much more easy and supportable.

Besides there is no occasion to fear that the Narration of all these tragical Accidents should offend the Ears of your Eminence, or disturb the Sweetness and Goodness of your Nature: That complete Knowledge you have acquired in Politicks, that long Practice and Experience that you have had in the Courts of the greatest Monarchs where these *Machiavelianisms* are so common, will not permit any one to imagine that you have any thing to learn concerning them. And farther, altho' Justice and Clemency are two Virtues very becoming a great Man, yet it is not always requisite that he should have the same inclination to Pity, for which *Seneca* gives this Reason in his Treatise of Clemency, (*Book* 2. *ch.* 5.) *Quemadmodum Religio Deos colit, superstitio violat, Clementiam Mansuetudinemque omnes boni præstabunt, misericordiam autem vitabunt, est enim vitium pusilli animi ad speciem alienorum malorum subsidentis;* As Religion worships the Gods, Superstition profanes them, so all good Men will shew Clemency and Mercy, but will avoid Pity, which is the Failure of a weak Mind, sinking under the appearance of other Mens Misfortunes: Now it would be a Crime to think, that there could be any thing in your Eminence that is low or abject, since if it be true which the same Author says, that *Nihil æque Homines ac magnis Animis decet,* Nothing is so becoming a Man as a great Spirit: With how much greater Reason ought that Spirit to appear in your Eminence, to accompany and heighten that Dignity you sustain, not only as a Prince of the Church, but as a chief Counsellor to his Holiness, and so in some measure of one of the most potent Princes of *Europe: Magnam enim fortunam Magnus animus decet qui nisi se ad illam extulit & altior stetit illam quoque infra terram deducit*; For a great Soul is proper for a great Fortune; for unless a Man carries himself beyond it and exalts himself higher, he draws it down with him and depresses it. At least it occasions the Management of it to have less Authority and Reputation. So we find in History, that *Epiphanes*, for having acted below his Dignity, and not governing like a King, was sirnam'd the *Insensible*, and that

Ramirus of *Arragon*, retaining several of his Monkish Manners, after having quitted the Convent, to take the Crown, was derided and contemn'd by his Courtiers; our own Times furnish us with the Examples of a King of *Great Britain*, who *E stato schernito, & besseggiato per haver voluto comporre libri & fare del letterato* (*Tassoni*, Book 7. c. 4.) was thought to act below his Dignity, by writing Books, and being learned: And of *Henry* III. so much spoke of, and so remarkable in our Modern Histories, who having liv'd amongst Monks, and through the excess of an ill-guided Devotion, abandon'd his Crown and Government, gave occasion to Pope *Sixtus* the Fifth to say, *This good King does all that he can to be a Monk, and I have done all that I could not to be one.* And for this reason, some of the best Advice that ever *Monsieur de Villeroy* gave to *Henry* the Great, who had liv'd like a Soldier and Musqueteer, during the Wars he made before his coming to the Crown, was, when he told him, *That a Prince, who was not jealous of the Respects due to his Majesty, would permit himself to be affronted and despised. That the Kings his Predecessors, in the utmost Confusions, had always acted like Kings: that it was time he should speak, write, and act like a King.*

But why should we search for Examples amongst strange Princes, when the History of those who have govern'd this City, in which your Eminence resides at present, shews us two Sovereign Popes, who not having accompany'd the Grandeur of their Supreme Dignity with an equal Spirit, serve still for the Subject of Tales and Raillery, and of Laughter to Posterity. The great Piety and Religion which they carried in their Countenance, not being able to hinder, but that *Masson* should say of the first, who was *Celestin* the Fifth, *Vir fuit simplex nec eruditus, qui humana negotia ne capere quidem posset.* He was a simple Man, no Scholar, and one that had no Apprehension of common Business. And *Paulus Jovius* speaking of the second, concerning a certain sort of Fish, which rose to a great Price during his Pontificate, *Merluceo plebeio admodum pisci, Hadrianus sextus sicuti in republica administranda hebetis ingenii vel depravati judicii, ita in esculentis insulsissimi gustus, supra mediocre pretium ridente toto foro Piscatorio jam fecerat.* (Lib. de Pisc. Rom.) That he shew'd himself to be as dull, and of as depraved a Judgment in his Administration of Affairs, as he was insipid in his Taste. In which Character he shew'd himself to be as dull, and of as depraved a Judgment in his Administration of Affairs, as he was insipid in his Taste. In which Character he shew'd himself much more moderate than *Peter Martyr*, not the Heretick of *Florence*, but the Apostolick Protonatory, Native of a little Village in the Dutchy of *Milan*, who says of the Election of the same Pope, *Cardinalibus hoc loco accidit, quod in fabulis de Pardo ac Leone super Agno raptando scribitur, fortibus illis strenue se dilacerantibus quodcumque quadrupes iners aliud prædæ se dominum fecit;* Whilst the Leopard and Lyon were fighting for the Lamb, a stupid Beast ran away with the Prey: So that Persons shou'd either avoid great Employments, or else administer them with a Generosity and Force of Spirit, so far exalted above what is common, that it may be able to make Fortune desire to second and favour it in all Undertakings. This being a most certain Maxim, that whoever has this Principle and Foundation, which comes by Nature, *Bona enim mens, nec emitur, nec comparatur*, says *Seneca,* for a good Understanding is not to be bought or traffick'd for, cannot miss of being the Worker and Creator of his own Fortune, according to *Plautus, Sapiens pol ipse fingit fortunam sibi. Alexander,* although he was young, and ill provided with Soldiers, propos'd to himself to conquer the *Persians,* and pass even to the *Indies,* and accomplish'd it: *Cæsar* undertook in his single Person, to govern that Republick which commanded all others, he found the means of doing it: The two Shepherds, *Romulus* and *Tamerlane,* had their Designs to lay the Foundation of two powerful Empires, and they executed them. *Mahomet,* from a Merchant, would make himself a Prophet, and from a Prophet, a Sovereign of the third part of the World; he had Success. And what think you, my Lord, was the principal Spring which caus'd all these marvellous Effects? No other in truth but a valiant Mind, which *Juvenal* teaches us always to place among the foremost of our Desires, *Fortem posce animum.* Now in this place to specifie the Parts that compose this Noble Spirit, would be to fall from one Discourse to another, and do as *Montagne,* who follows rather the Starts of his own Fancy, than the Titles of his Essays. It may be sufficient to say at present, that one of the first and most necessary things, is, often to recollect this Saying of *Seneca, O quam contempta res est homo nisi supra humana surrexerit*; Oh what a despicable Thing is Man, unless he raises himself above human Things; that is, unless he have a strong and fix'd Eye, and, as if he were plac'd upon some high Tower, looks down upon the whole World, which appears to him as a Theatre, ill regulated, and full of Confusion, where some act Comedies, and others Tragedies, and where he may intervene; *Tanquam Deus aliquis ex machina,* Like some Divinity from a Machine, as often as he pleases, or the variety of Occasions shall persuade him to do it. Now if it may seem extraordinary to your Eminence, and not proper for my Age, or perhaps my Condition, that I should be so resolute in Matters that are so ticklish and delicate, and much more in the Mouth of a young Man, who is call'd by *Horace, Utilium tardus provisor,* as being too negligent in providing such things as may be useful hereafter, and not accustom'd to apply himself to so serious and important Studies, which belong to the fulness of old Age. I shall first answer your Eminence, that the Age in which I am, is not disproportion'd to the Matter and Subject which I treat of; for Youth, that is, *Optima quæque dies,* &c. as *Virgil* and *Seneca* call it, has that Epithet of *Best,* because the Mind is tractable, and the Time fitted for Labour, and proper to be exercis'd in fitting Studies. Why then, since several Persons have perform'd many brave Exploits before the Flower of their Age, should not I be permitted to follow them, and if not to produce generous and lofty Actions, at least to frame noble and bold Conceptions, seeing I have always endeavour'd to acquire certain good Dispositions of Mind, which ought not now to be unuseful to me: For I have address'd my self to the Muses, without being too much enamour'd of them; I was pleas'd with my Studies, but not too much addicted to them; I pass'd through a Course of Scholastic Philosophy, without medling with the contentious parts of it, and thorough that of the Ancients and Moderns, without being partial to any Sect; I made more use of *Seneca* than *Aristotle,* of *Plutarch* than *Plato,* of *Juvenal* and *Horace,* than *Homer* and *Virgil,* and of *Montagn* and *Charon*, more than all the before-mention'd. I have not had so much practice of the World, as effectually to discover the Cheats and Villanies that are committed in it, but I have nevertheless seen a great part of them, in Histories, Satyrs and Tragedies. Pedantry might have gained something upon my Behaviour and Carriage, during seven or eight Years that I staid in the Colleges, but I can assure my self, that it obtained no Advantage over my Spirit; Nature, God be prais'd, has been no Stepmother to me, and the reading of divers Authors has given me great Assistance, but that of the *Book* of St. *Antoine*, has furnish'd me with the best. After all, I hope it may not displease your Eminence, that being full of Zeal and good Affection for your Service, I employ my Thoughts to give you any agreeable Diversion; but my last Design is, for a contemplative State of Life, to which I have vow'd, and design'd all the rest of my Days, without encumbring my self with the active, only so far as your Eminence, to whom I have made the first Vow of Obedience may please to engage me.

It remains now to see, if I do not pass beyond the Bounds of my Capacity, by endeavouring to treat of things that seem to be beyond my Knowledge; to which I may answer, with that of *Seneca, Paucis ad bonum mentem opus est literis,* There is not much Learning requir'd to a good Understanding. I have not the Presumption to think I shall obtain the Prize in this Course, I shall only make a small Effort, and when I am out of the right way, I shall expect some new Assistance or Instruction to pass farther. *Arastus*, that excellent Man, who did not understand much of Astronomy, yet made a good Book of the *Phænomena's:* *Celsus*, who was a mere Grammarian, compos'd a most useful Book in Physick: *Dioscorides* was a Soldier, *Macer* a Senator, and yet both have writ very exquisitely concerning Plants: *Hippodamus*, from a simple Architect and Mason, became a great Politician, and Founder of a Commonwealth, that is mention'd by *Aristotle.* I have always been of this Opinion, that whoever has natural Parts, and some Improvement from study, may infer and deduce all sorts of Conclusions, from five or six good Principles, as *Pliny* says, That the ancient Painters made their best Pieces from the mixture only of four or five sorts of Colours; one may likewise add, that the Sciences seem to be link'd to one another, and to have such a Correspondence, that he who is possess'd of one, is likewise Master of all that stand in a Subaltern degree to it: Besides, the Age in which we live, seems much to favour this Design, since one may know and discover the greatest Secrets of Monarchies, the Intrigues of Courts, the Cabals of the Factious, the Pretences and Motives of particular Persons,

> *Quid Rex in aurem Reginæ dixerit,*
> *Quid Juno fabulata sit cum Jove.* (Plaut.)

what the King whisper'd to the Queen, what *Juno* discours'd of with *Jupiter*, by the means of so many Relations, Memoires, Discourses, Instructions, Libels, Manifesto's, Pasquinades, and such like secret Pieces that come abroad daily, which may more easily form and enliven our Minds and set us free from foolish Prejudice, than all the Actions that are usually practis'd in Courts of Princes, whose importance it is difficult to know, for want of being able to penetrate into their Causes and different Movements.

As for my own Method of treating this Subject, I shall do it with all the Precaution and Modesty imaginable; not minding the vulgar Notions, but such as the venerable *Cato* or *Curius* wou'd have fram'd: And if I knew in the least, that what I should say on this Subject, wou'd create any Abuse or Disorder, greater than what is this day practis'd among Princes, I wou'd throw these Papers into the Fire, and make an eternal Vow of Silence; for I wou'd not gain the Reputation of a subtle Politick Speculator, to lose that of an honest Man; which shall be the chief and only end I shall aim at in pursuing this Discourse.

CHAP. II. What are properly refin'd Politicks, and how many Sorts there are of them.

BUT that we may not still continue in these Preambles, let us come to the Subject which they are to introduce. That great Person *Justus Lipsius* treating of Prudence in his Book of Politicks, describes it in these few Words, *to be a Choice and Trial of such things as are to be avoided or desired*; and after having discoursed of it in the ordinary Method of the Schools, that is to say, as a Moral Virtue which has the Consideration of Good for its object, he afterwards comes to another Prudence which he calls mix't, because it is not so pure, so sound and consummate as the former, but partakes a little of those Arts and Stratagems which are commonly made use of in the Courts of Princes, and the Management of the most important Affairs of Government: and then he endeavours, by his Eloquence, to make it appear that this sort of Prudence, may be esteemed honest, and may be practis'd as being allowable and lawful. After which he describes it judiciously enough to be *Argutum Consilium a Virtute, aut Legibus devium, Regni Regisque bono:* A quick or sharp Advice deviating from Virtue and the Laws for the Good of the State or Prince. And then passing on to its several Kinds and differences, he constitutes three Principal ones, The first of which one may call a Trick or Deceit, that is, but slight and of small Consideration, which comprehends under it Distrust and

Dissimulation: The second retains something of Virtue but yet less of it than the former, and has for its Parts Conciliation and Deception, that is to say, the Method of gaining the Friendship and Service of some particular Persons, and the deluding, deceiving and drawing in of others, by false Promises, Flatteries, Presents, and other Baits, which may be said to be rather necessary than honest. As to the last, he says it is wholly estranged from Law and Virtue, and plunges deeper into Wickedness, and that its two Foundations or Bases are Treachery and Injustice.

However it seems to me, that to search particularly into the nature of these Secrets of State, and strike immediately upon the main Point of our Discourse, as to that which is proper and essential to them, we must consider *Prudence* as a Moral and Political Vertue, which has no other end than to find out the different Turns, the best and easiest Contrivances of managing and accomplishing that Design which a Man proposes; from whence it likewise follows that as these Affairs and Methods can be but of two sorts, one easie and ordinary, the other troublesome, difficult and extraordinary; so there are but two sorts of Prudence, the first ordinary and easie, which keeps the beaten Path, without exceeding the Laws and Customs of the Country: the second extraordinary, being rigorous and severe.

The first takes in all the Parts of Prudence, of which the Philosophers us'd to speak in their Moral Treatises, together with those three first above mentioned, which *Justus Lipsius* only assigns to the Prudence mixt with Fraud.

For to say the Truth, if one considers well the Necessity that Politicians have of them, to serve their own Purposes, we ought never to suppose them to be unjust or dishonest. For the better Understanding of this, we ought to know, as *Charon* says, (*Book 3. Ch.2.*) that the Justice, Virtue and Probity of a Sovereign moves in a different Sphere from that of particular Persons, and takes a larger and freer Compass from the Grandeur, Wightiness and Danger of his Burthen; and for this reason it is fitting that he take such steps as seem irregular and unpractis'd, yet to him are requisite and lawful; sometimes it is necessary to use Shifts and Evasions, and to mix Prudence with Justice, and as they say, *Cum Vulpe junctum Vulpinarier*; To play the Fox with the Fox: and in this consists the Art of Government.

Agents, Nuncioes, Embassadors and Legats are sent not only to pry into the Actions of Foreign Princes, but to dissemble, cover and disguise those of their own Masters. *Louis* the Eleventh, the best advis'd and wisest of our Kings, held this for a principal Maxim of his Government, that, *qui nescit dissimulare nescit regnare*, He who does not know how to dissemble, knows not how to reign. The Emperor *Tiberius, Nullam ex Virtutibus suis magis quam dissimulationem deligebat*, preferr'd his Dissimulation to all his other Accomplishments. And is it not apparent that the greatest Virtue reigning now at Court is to distrust all the World and dissemble with every body; seeing they who are plain and open are no ways fit for the Mystery of Government, and often bring themselves and the State into danger. But not only these two Parts of Distrust and Dissimulation which consist in Omission, when properly applied are necessary to Princes; but is often requisite to pass farther, and to come to Action: As for example, to gain some Advantage or to accomplish some secret Design by Equivocation and Subtilty, to sooth with soft Words, fine Letters, specious Embassies, obtaining by those Artifices such things as the Difficulty of their Circumstances might otherwise have made them despair of, *Et si recte portum tenere nequeas idipsum mutata velificatione assequi;* (Cicero *Book* 2. *to* Lentulus) So that if you cannot arrive at the Port by direct sailing, by veering about you may accomplish it. It is likewise necessary to have Intrigues and secret Correspondences, so as to win the Hearts and Affections of the Officers, Servants and Confidents of other Princes, foreign Persons of Quality and even of their own Subjects, this is what *Cicero* calls in the first of his Offices, *Conciliare sibi animos hominum & ad suos usus adjungere.* What Necessity therefore is there of setting up a particular Prudence by the Name of mixt, on which such Actions should depend, as *Justus Lipsius* does; since they all come under the Head of *Ordinary Prudence*: and such Artifices are every Day taught by the Politicians, urg'd in their Arguments, enforc'd by their Ministers, and practis'd without any Suspicion of Injustice as being the principal Rules and Maxims for the well governing of States and Empires. These deserve not so much to be call'd the *Secrets of Government*, the *Fine-spun Politicks*, and the *Arcana Imperiorum*, as those others which are comprehended under the last sort of *Extraordinary Prudence*, which gives a turn to the most intricate and difficult Affairs; which more particularly and with Exclusion to all others should have the Name of *Arcana Imperiorum*, and this Title they have not only from me, but from all other preceding Authors.

And here we may take notice of a Fault in a great many of them who have treated of Politicks, and particularly of *Clapmarius*, who making a large Book, *De Arcanis Imperiorum*, and reducing them under some general Precepts, says in the first place, that *Secrets* of *State* are nothing else but the various Methods, Reasons and Counsels which Princes make use of to maintain their Authority and the State of the Publick, without transgressing common Right, or giving any suspicion of Fraud and Injustice. This being pre-suppos'd as true and certatin, he divides them into two sorts, and says, the first ought to be called the *Secrets of Empire or of Republicks*, and these by reason of the three sorts of Government he subdivides into six others: So that for Example, A Monarchy ought to have its Schemes and peculiar Reasons of State to preserve it from being commanded by such as would reduce it to an *Aristocracy*, and others likewise to hinder it from falling into the hands of the People, and becoming a *Democracy*. And so the two others ought to take care least they become Monarchies, or be chang'd into that other Form of Government that is opposite to them. The second sort are those to which he gives the Title of *Secrets of Dominion*, which they who Rule are oblig'd to practise for the Preservation of their Authority, whether it be Monarchical, Popular or Aristocratical; which he illustrates by a curious enumeration of all those instances he has gather'd from *Livy, Salust, Ammianus Marcellinus*, and several other Authors, who seem all to agree as to the signification of these *Terms*, in the same manner as he himself has us'd them.

I might incur the Displeasure of such great Men, if I did not first ask Pardon for my Freedom, in telling them that the usage of the words *Secrets of State*, according to the before-mention'd Exposition, is to deviate from their true Signification, and not to comprehend the nature of the Thing; it being certain that these Latin words *Secretum* and *Arcanum*, which they have made use of, cannot be appropriated to the Precepts and Maxims of a Science, which is commonly understood and practised by ever one: But only to that, which for some Reasons ought neither to be known or divulg'd, because according to that Remark of the Poet *Marbodæus* (Book of Gemms).

Non secreta manent quorum fit conscia turba.

They are no *Secrets* which the Vulgar know.

We likewise learn from the Grammarians, that this Word *Arcanum* may be deriv'd from *Arce*, a *strong Tower*, either because as *Festus Pompeius* asserts, the *Augurs* had a Custom to offer a certain Sacrifice there, which they would hide from the Knowledge of the People, or because all things Secret and of Consequence are better secur'd in *Arce*, such a *Fortress*, than in any other Place. Those who derive it from *Arca*, a *Coffer*, seem likewise not to differ in Opinion; and all good Authors never use these two Words but in a like signification.

Longius & Volvens Fatorum Arcana movebo,
(Virg. Æn. I.

——From far
I'll fetch the Secrets of revolving Fates.

And in another place,

Te colere, Arcanos etiam tibi credere sensus.

Adore and trust thee with my *secret* Soul.

And *Horace* has

Secretumq; teges & Vino tortus & ira.

And keep a Secret tho' much Wine and Rage
Should put thee on the Rack.

And to conclude with that of *Lucan*, speaking of the Source of *Nile*, which was wholly unknown to the *Ægyptians* themselves,

Arcanum Natura caput non protulit ulli
Nec licuit populis parvum te Nile videre
Amovitq; sinus, & Gentes maluit ortus
Mirari quam nosse tuos.

Nature, oh *Nile*, thy secret Head to none,
Nor infant Streams has to the vulgar show,

> But far remov'd the Beds from which you flow,
> Whilst Men admire that Birth they ne'er shall know.

I cannot but Remark that a beautiful Parallel may be drawn between the River *Nile* and the *Secrets of State*; for as the Nations that bordered upon that Current receiv'd a thousand Advantages from it, without knowing whence it took its rise; so the People ought to admire the happy effects of these master strokes of Policy, though wholly ignorant of those Causes from whence they result.

Now having shewn that these Writers have corrupted the Word, we may likewise say they have in like manner deprav'd the Nature of the thing, seeing they propose to us general Precepts and universal Maxims, founded upon the Justice and Right of Sovereignty, and consequently not only permitted, but every Day practis'd in the sight of all the World, which they however look upon as *Secrets of State*. Nor do they consider that there is a great difference between these and those others we speak of, since everyone is capable of knowing the first by a slight Study of the Authors that treat of them; whereas on the contrary, the latter, concerning which the Question now arises, have their birth in the most retir'd Cabinets of Princes, and are not handled or deliberated in a full Senate, but between two or three of the most able and finish'd Ministers that a Prince has about him.

Of this we have an Example in *Augustus*, who, when he had a design after his Victory at *Actium,* and the conclusion of all his Wars both at home and abroad, to quit the Title of

Emperor, and give Liberty to his Country, did not communicate it to the Senate, though he had increas'd their Number by six hundred Senators, nor to his particular Council which was compos'd of Twenty Persons the most accomplish'd and Judicious that he could chuse; but he propos'd and committed this whole Affair to the Judgment of his two principal Friends, Ministers and Confidents, *Mecænas* and *Agrippa*; *Quibuscum Imperii Arcana communicare solebat;* to whom he us'd to communicate the Secrets of his Empire, as *Dion* tells us *Book* 53.

And if we look upwards to the great Man that was his Predecessor, we shall find that *Julius Cæsar,* as *Suetonius* delivers it in his Life, had only *Quintus Pedius* and *Cornelius Balbus*, to whom he communicated τα μυσικάτατα, that is, the very Secrets of his Soul. The *Lacedæmonians,* whose State was much enlarg'd after the Victory gain'd by *Lysander,* did thereupon with great Prudence establish a Council of Thirty Persons to preside over the Affairs of the Commonwealth; but not content with that they chose Twelve of the most judicious and experienc'd of their Citizens to be, as it were, their Oracle; whose Answers were to be to them conclusive in their *finest strokes* of Policy. The *Venetians* do the same at this Day with their *Procurators* of St. *Mark*; and there is no Sovereign how weak soever, and inconsiderate he may be, that can be so ill advis'd as to remit that to the Judgment of the Publick, which can scarce remain secret enough in the Ear of a Minister or Favourite. Which made *Cassiodorus* say, *Arduum nimis est Principis meruisse secretum,* (*Book* 8. *Ep.* 10.) It is too sublime a thing to deserve a Prince's Secret.

And in another place, where he speaks of a Favourite of *Theodoric's, Tecum pacis certa tecum Belli dubia conferebat, & quod apud sapientes Reges singulare munus est ille sollicitus ad omnia, Tecum pectoris pandebat Arcana,* (Book 8, Ep. 9.) With you he conferr'd in the doubtful Cases both of Peace and War, and gave you that Favour which is very signal amongst wise Princes; for after all his Care for Publick Affairs, he disburthen'd his Secrets in your Breast. It would have look'd very well if *Charles* the Ninth had consulted all the Counsellors of his Parliament concerning what was to be done upon the Feast of St *Bartholomew*, or *Henry* the Third had determin'd the Death of the *Guises* at the Council Board. They would have succeeded as well as if they would have taken Hares by Beat of Drum, and Birds by the Sound of Trumpets.

Besides, I would willingly ask these Gentlemen if they call the common Rules of governing Kingdoms, the *Arcana Imperiorum*, what Name they would give to those *Secrets* which are mixt with some Severity, and have occasion for extraordinary Prudence, which we are going now to mention. For to call them as *Clapmarius* does after *Tacitus*, the *Flagitia Imperiorum*, is rather to take notice of those that are done in consideration of some private Advantage by some Tyrant, than of many others which are transacted for the publick Interest, and with all the Equity that can be applied to Enterprizes of such Importance, which nevertheless cannot be so well circumstantiated as not to be accompanied by some piece of Injustice, and consequently may be subject to Blame and Calumny.

These words being so explain'd, let us pass to the Nature of the thing signified by them: Now the better to comprehend this, it is necessary to search farther back, and to shew how in a retir'd Life and the government of a Man's self, and in the OEconomy or Conduct of a Family, which are two diminutive sorts of Politicks, there are several Subtilties, Feints and Stratagems which many make daily use of to come at the height of their Pretensions. *Charon* in his Book of Wisdom, *Cardan* in his Works, entituled, *Proxeneta, de Utilitate capienda ex adversis*, and *de Sapientia, Matchiavel* in his Discourses upon *Livy*, and in his *Prince,* have laid down Precepts at large concerning those matters. As for my self, it will be sufficient to bring some Examples from them, after having observ'd, that although *Justus Lipsius* (*Civ. Doctr.* Book 4. c. 14.) has said of the last, *Ab illo facile obtinebimus, nec Maculonem Italum tam districte dammandum (qui misera qua non manu hodie vapulat) & esse quamdam ut vire sanctus aid* (Basil in Proverb.) καλήν κ, ἐπαινετήν πανουργίαν, *Honestam atque laudabilem calliditatem.* We shall easily bring him to grant, that the *Italian* Disturber, who at present is lash'd by every body, is not to be so severely blam'd, seeing as St. *Basil* says, there is a Craft that is honest and commendable. And tho' *Gaspar Schioppius* has wrote a little Tract in his Defence, yet I cannot but be something offended at him, because

> ——*Floribus Austrum*
> *Perditus, & liquidis immisit fontibus Apros.*
> (Virg. Bucol. Ecl. 2.)

The Boar amidst the chrystal Streams I bring,

And Southern Winds to blast my flow'ry Spring,

as Mr. *Dryden* has express'd it in the first Person, by being the first that was so bold to advance his Steps, break the Ice, and as I may so say, profan'd that by his Writings which the most judicious made use of as the hidden and prevailing Means to accomplish their Designs. I might make some scruple of adding any thing to what he had said, if the Persons above nam'd, and others that treat of Politicks had not done the same before me, and now and then given occasion to say in this matter, what *Juvenal* said of Poetry.

> *—Stulta est Clementia, cum tot ubique*
> *Vatibus occurras, perituræ percere chartæ.*
> Sat. I.

> But since the World with writing is possess'd,
> I'll versifie in spite, and do my best
> To make as much waste Paper as the rest.
> Mr. *Dryden.*

Now amongst the Secrets which regard particular Persons, I cannot think there are any of a higher reach, with regard to the End aimed at, than those which have been practis'd by certain Persons, who would distinguish themselves from the rest of Mankind, by establishing amongst them an Opinion of their Divinity: So we see that *Salmoneus* fram'd a Bridge of Brass, over which he drew his Chariot with high mettled Horses, and darting artificial Fires from both his Hands, imagin'd that he could imitate the Lightning and

Thunder of *Jupiter*, from whence the Poet took occasion to say

> *Vidi & Crudeles dantem Salmonea pœnas,*
> *Dum flammas Jovis & sonitus imitatur Olympi.*
> Virg. Æn. 6.

> *Salmoneus* suffering cruel Pains I found,
> For emulating *Jove*, the ratling Sound
> Of Mimick Thunder, and the glitt'ring Blaze.
> Of pointed Lightning, and their forked Rays.
> Mr. *Dryden*.

Psapho, who was not less ambitious than the former, bred up a great number of *Jays, Sterlings, Magpies, Parrots*, and other Birds, and having taught them to pronounce these Words, *Psapho* is a God, let them fly abroad at Liberty, that such Persons as heard these extraordinary Witnesses of his Divinity, might the more easily be induced to believe it: So *Heraclides Ponticus*, having commanded one of his Servants that he could best confide in, to hide a great Serpent, bred for that Design, under the Coverings that were over him when he went to be buried, that the Creature, disturbed by the Noise they would make, might leap out amongst the Mourners, and give the common People reason to believe that he was deify'd. As for *Empedocles*, he proceeded with that Courage and Generosity which became a Philosopher, for being grown old, and loaded with Glory and Honour, he threw himself into the flaming *Volcano's* of *Ætna*, to make Men believe he was taken up into Heaven, as a *Romulus* did by drowning himself in a Marsh.

——Deus immortalis haberi
Dum cupit Empedocles ardentem frigidus Ætnam
Insiluit.   Hor. Art. Poet.

Empedoces for an immortal Name,
Sedately ventures into *Ætna*'s Flame.

The Atheists, who make their Glosses upon all the Texts of Holy Scripture, think that of *Deuteronomy*, Chap. 34. ought to be understood after the same manner, and that *Moses* threw himself from some Precipice into an Abyss, that the *Jews* might think he was taken into Heaven, whereas they ought rather to believe and agree with the Christians, that his Body was hid, least the *Jews* should idolize it after his Death, it being well known that they were inclin'd, not only naturally, but from their Conversation with the *Ægyptians*, to adore all those from whom they had received any Benefit, or whose Virtue they imagin'd to have been singular and extraordinary.

The same Judgment may be made of the Golden Thigh of *Pythagoras*, mention'd by *Diogenes Laertius*, seeing *Plutarch* plainly tells us in the Life of *Numa*, that it was only a Contrivance and Stratagem of the Philosopher, to establish in his Admirers an Opinion of his Divinity; but what *Hercules* did was very much more ingenious, for being conversant in Astrology, as the Story of his Life shews sufficiently, when it says he bore up the Heavens in the room of *Atlas*, he chose exactly the Time and Hour when a great Comet was to appear, to set Fire to that Pile in which he resolv'd to end his Days, that this Celestial Fire might come in as a Witness, and make the same thing be believed concerning him, which the *Romans* would persuade the People to think concerning some of their Emperors, by the means of an Engle let fly from the midst of the Flames of their Funeral Pile, that the soul of the deceas'd was carried into the Arms of *Jupiter*.

Many others who were more modest and reserv'd in their Designs, were content to let us know the Care that the Gods took of their Persons, by the continual Assistance of some Genius or particular Divinity; this was done among the Ancients, by *Socrates, Pliny, Porphyry, Brutus, Sylla* and *Apollonius*, not to mention several Legislators; and amongst the Moderns, *Picus Mirandula, Cecco d'Ascoli, Hermolaus, Savanarola, Niphus, Postellus, Cardan* and *Campanella*, who boasted that they had such an Attendant, and that he convers'd with them, and yet they were never accus'd of having practis'd the Theurgick Ceremonies, contain'd in a Book falsly attributed to *Virgil, De videndo Genio*, or the *Means how to see a Genius*, or mention'd by *Arbatel*, in an undigested Collection out of such like Books, which is falsly publish'd under the Name of *Agrippa*. As for my self, I should rather endeavour to establish the truth of these Stories, by the wonderful Force of the Contraction of the Spirits, so well explain'd by *Marsilius Ficinus*, and *Jurdanus Brunus,*, from which *Palingenius* does not seem much to differ in three or four places of his *Zodiaque*; unless we would rather choose to say that these Gentlemen acted the Impostors, and would imitate the Stories of *Numa, Zamolxis* and *Minos*, or rather, those which the Rabbies and Cabalists

(*Reuchlin Lib. de Cabala*) have pleasantly forg'd concerning the Patriarchs of the Old Testament, and would make us believe that *Adam* was govern'd by his Angel *Raziel, Sem* by *Jophiel, Abraham* by *Frza-d-Kiel, Isaac* by *Raphael, Jacob* by *Piel*, and *Moses* by *Mittaron, —Sed credat Judaeus Apella, non Ego; Let the Jews believe it, I sha'n't.* However, this may be remark'd of the Historians, that these Contrivances have not always been without their Use, seeing *Scipio* practising them with Judgment amongst the *Romans*, acquir'd the Reputation of a great and good Man, and was sent to conquer *Spain*, though he was not then of the Age of four and twenty: *Livy* speaks thus concerning him; *Fuit Scipio non tantum veris artibus mirabilis, sed arte quoque quadam adinventa ad ostentationem composita pleraque apud multitudinem aut per nocturnas visas species, aut veluti divinitus mente monita agens; Scipio* was not only admirable for his true Politicks, but likewise for his artificial Contrivances, transacting many things with the Populace, as proceeding from Nocturnal Appearances, or the influence of some Divine Admonition: So likewise many other Princes and private Men, that were not capable of arriving at the Fineness of such Inventions, contented themselves with something else, that they thought might contribute to the Lustre of their Actions. 'Tis for this reason *Tacitus* says, that *Vespasian* was, *Omnium quæ diceret aut ageret arte quadam Ostentator*, had a certain Art of setting off all he said or did, with a sort of Ostentation, (*Annals Book* 3.) and *Corbulo* is represented by the same Author, *Super experientiam sapientiamque etiam specie inanium validus*, besides his Wisdom and Experience, he made even trifling Appearances become prevalent; and this was done for a good Reason, since he says in another place, *Principibus omnia ad famam dirigenda*, Princes should direct all their Actions to the obtaining a Reputation, seeing, according to *Cardan's* Remark, *Æstimatio & opinio rerum humanarum Reginæ sunt,* (Book 3. *De Util.*) for Esteem and Opinion are the Queens of Human Actions. Several other Observations which relate to the government of particular Persons might here be made, but for those I shall refer to the Treatise of *Cardan* just now cited, and proceed to the Secrets of OEconomy, or the Rule and Administration of Families, in which I content my self with taking notice of some that have been used to counterplot the Intrigues which Women make use of against their Husbands, in their pursuit of unlawful Pleasures; to which purpose I remember to have read a Story in the pleasant Tales of *Bouchet*, or *Chaudrier*, which shall here pass for serious, as being much more proper to correct these wanton Humours, than that of *La Mule*, who was eight Days without drinking, which is mention'd by *Cardan* in his *Book of Wisdom*. A certain Pysician, say they, being inform'd that his Wife went to divert her self,

> *Intrabat calidum veteri Centone Lupanar,*
> Juvenal.

Would often go to Places of no very good Credit, and that the next Day she was to meet Company, was not in the least concern'd at it nor took any notice, but at midnight, and when his Wife dreamt of nothing less, leapt out of Bed feigning that Thieves were in the House, takes his Sword in his Hands, discharges two or three Pistols, cries *Help,*

Murder, strikes his Sword upon the Table and Wainscot, in short, does all he could to frighten and disturb his Family; In the morning when all was over, he felt his Wife's Pulse, and found it much oppres'd by reason of the fright she had had, and for that he must take away ten or twelve Ounces of Blood. Now this Evacuation having caus'd a small Emotion, he began to seem concerned as if she had a high Fever, upon which he repeated the bleeding seven or eight times afterwards, he proceeded to shaving cupping and purging her to the last degree, so that she kept her Bed six Months, without ever having been sick. In the mean time, he had opportunity to ruin her Intrigues and break off her old Acquaintance, to spoil her fine Complexion, cool her warm Blood, allay the Ferment of the Humours, which had rais'd in her a Flame more unextinguishable than that of the Stone *Asbestos,*

Qui nulla moritur, nullaque extinguitur Arte.
(Trigault.)

That cannot die, nor yet be quench'd by Art.

But the Secrets the People of *China* practise to cure those Disorders which are crept into Families is much neater and more artful. For they have made it one of the principal Laws of their Nation, That the chief Grace and Beauty of their Women should depend upon the smallness of their Feet, and that they should be esteemed the most beautiful who had the smallest and prettiest. This Law was no sooner publish'd, but all the Mothers, without considering the consequence, began to swath and bind up their

Daughters Feet so tight, that they could not go abroad, nor indeed stand upright, but by the assistance of two or three Servants, so this Figure, tho' at first artificial, passing into a natural Shape, like that of the *Macrocephali* or People with *long Heads,* mention'd by *Hippocrates,* the *Chinese* insensibly fix'd the Mercury which their Women had in their Feet, making them resemble the *Tortoise* mention'd by the Poets.

——Tardigrada & domiporta
Sub pedibus Veneris *Cous quam finxit* Apelles.

Of Progress slow, with House upon her Back,
Such as *Apelles* plac'd at *Venus*'s Feet.

By this means they hindred them from walking abroad with their Gallants, and to their usual Appointments: In the same manner as the *Venetian* Ladies are oblig'd to stay at home much oftner than they would do, by the use and extraordinary inconvenience of their *Choppins*: But the Story reported by *Mocquet* is much stranger and surprizing, for he says, that he has not only been credibly informed, but has seen it practis'd amongst the *Caribes* a People rude and barbarous, that when a Husband dies, let it be by what accident soever, the Woman is constrain'd under pain of remaining contemptible, infamous and deserted by all her Friends and Relations, to resolve to die with him to throw her self into a great Pile of Fire, with as much Pomp and rejoycing as if it were upon the day of her Nuptials: upon which *Mocquet* says, that being much surpriz'd, he ask'd the reason of such a Custom, and was answer'd, that this was wisely establish'd as a Remedy for the great Inconstancy and Falseness of the Women of this Country, who before the making of this Law were used to poison their Husbands when they were weary of them, or had a mind to marry some other that was more strong and vigorous,

Quique suo melius nervum tendebat Ulysse.

Who than *Ulysses* drew a stronger Bow.

Now if this Remedy was well proportion'd to the Nature of those People for whom it was ordain'd, that which *Dionysius* the Tyrant of *Syracuse* put in practice to hinder the Feasts and Assemblies which were kept in the Night, was not less fitted to his Occasions; for without declaring that they any way displeas'd him, or showing that he feared lest they had any design to conspire against him, he was content by degrees to grant Impunity to all Riots and Thefts that were committed in the Night, turning them into a Subject of Laughter, and by this Connivance gave such a Confidence to all the loose Fellows in the Town to use all People ill that they met in the Streets, in the night time, that no Person durst stir out of their House after Sun set, for fear of running the hazard of being stript or murder'd by those sorts of Robbers.

Let us come now to some others, less serious and consequently less troublesome and dangerous: The Republicks of *Greece* being desirous that their Subjects should eat their Fish whilst it was fresh and at a reasonable

Rate, had not recourse to the Methods of laying a Fine upon them, for which the Fishmongers might have had some reason to complain, but they took the Advice which the Comick Poet *Alexis* says was proposed to them by *Aristonicus*, they laid a grievous Penalty upon all Persons that sold Fish if they did sit down in the Market, *Ut ii standi tædio lassitudineq; confecti, quam recentissimos venderent;* That being weary of standing they might sell them fresh to dispatch their Market: So the *Romans* would not suffer the Priests of *Jupiter* to ride on Horse-back, lest as *Festus Pompius* says, *Si longius urbe discederent, sacra negligerentur;* If they should go far from the City the Holy Offices might chance to be neglected.

It were an easie thing to produce several more Examples of this kind, if these were not sufficient to let us judge of the rest, and to lead us to the third sort, which is that of Politicks, or the Government of Nations by one Person or by man: Now in relation to this last, that nothing may be omitted that can serve for its Illustration, we may observe three things; The first is the general Science of the Establishment and Preservation of States and Empires, which Science does not only contain what has been delivered down to us by *Plato* and *Aristotle*, but likewise all that *Tully* in his Book of Laws, *Xenophon* in his Prince, *Plutarch* in his Maxims, *Isocrates, Synesius* and other Authors have thought necessary to be understood and practis'd b those who govern: It is likewise certain, that it consists in many Rules that are universally received and approv'd, such as these; That things do not happen by chance or necessity; That there is a God that is the first

Cause of all things, who has made a Heaven for the Reward of the Just, and eternal Torments for the Punishment of the Wicked; That some ought to command, and others to obey; That it is the Duty of a Man to defend his Religion, his Prince and his Country, in the sight of all Men, and against all Men; That the main Strength of a Prince consists in the Love and Union of his Subjects; That he has a right to levy Money from his Subjects to supply the Necessities of War, and for the Maintenance of his Court, with several others set forth and explained by *Marni, Ammirato, Paruta, Remigio, Fiorentino, Zinaro, Malvezzi,* and *Botero* in their Political Discourses.

The second is properly what the *French* call *Maximes d'Estat*, and the *Italians Ragion di Stato*, though *Boterus* has compris'd all the three Differences under that Term, when he says, *Ragione di State e notitia di Mezzi atti a fundare, conservare & ampliare, un Dominio*, Reason of State is the Knowledge of measures proper for the Foundation, Preservation, and Increase of a Dominion; in which he has not hit so right, in my Opinion, as those who defin'd it to be, *Excessus juris communis propter commune Bonum*, An Encroaching upon common Right for the common Good; seeing this Definition being more special, particular and determinate, one may distinguish by it betwixt the first Rules for the Foundations of Empires, which are established upon Laws, and conformable to Reason; and these second which *Clapmarius* improperly calls *Arcana Imperiorum*, and we, with more reason, *Maxims of State*, since they cannot be pronounced Lawful, either according to the Natural or Civil Law, or the Laws of Nations but only out of Consideration of the publick Good, which often reaches father than that of particular Persons; so we see that *Claudius*, when by the Laws of his Country he could not take *Julia Agrippina* the Daughter of *Germanicus* to be his Wife, he had recourse to the Laws of State, and so found out an evident Contradiction to the ordinary ones, and married her, *ne fœmina expertæ fœcunditatis*, says *Tacitus, integra juventa, claritudinem Cæsarum in aliam domum transferret*, Book 12. That is to say, lest this Lady happening to marry into some great House, the Blood of the *Cæsars* might be spread into other Families, and produce a Number of Princes and Princesses, who in time might have some Pretensions to the Empire and consequently disturb the publick Tranquility. For the same reason *Tiberius* would not let *Agrippina* the Widow of *Germanicus*, and Mother to her we have been speaking of, marry again, tho' she required it of him with such Remonstrances, supported with powerful Reasons, as could not be refus'd her, without Injustice, which nevertheless was render'd lawful, by Reason of State, since *Tiberius* was not ignorant (*quantum ex republica peteretus, Tacitus* Book 4. Annal.) that is to say, what consequence this Marriage might be of, and that the Children which should spring from it, being so nearly related to *Augustus*, the *Roman* State might some Day fall into great Troubles and Parties by reason of divers Persons that might make Pretences to the Empire. No Law likewise permits us to procure the Ill and Disadvantage of one that never has done us any harm. And yet this Maxim of State related by *Livy* (Book 2. Dec. 5.) *Id agendum ne omnium rerum jus ac potestas ad unum populum perveniat*, That care should be taken that no one People should have an universal Power; obliges us to succour our Neighbour against those who have never offended us for fear their Ruin should serve as Steps to hasten our own, and that all our Companions being devoured b those new *Cyclops*'s, we should expect no other Favour than that which was granted to *Ulysses* to be the last Morsel to satisfie their Hunger. This is the Pretext that the *Ætolians* made use of to obtain Succours from King *Antiochus* and *Demetrius* King of the *Illyrians* to excite *Philip* King of *Macedonia* and Father of *Perseus* to take up Arms against the *Romans*. This was likewise the Reason why that great Politician *Cosmo de Medicis*, was so desirous to keep *Milan* from falling into the hands of the *Venetians*, when the Race of the *Visconti* Dukes of *Milan* was extinct. And *Henry* the *Fourth* being inform'd that the Duke of *Savoy* had fail'd in his Attempt to surprize *Geneva*, said openly, That if it had succeeded he would have laid Siege to it the Day following; and yet when the King of *Spain* invaded the same Duke's Territories, *France* upon the foremention'd Maxim, came in powerfully to his Assistance. It was this which furnish'd *Alexendar* the *Sixth* and *Francis* the *First* with a lawful Excuse for making Alliances with the Grant Seignior: From thence the *Spaniards* held a secret Correspondence with the *Hugonots*, and *France* let Troops pass privately into the *Valtoline* and into *Holland*, though all this seem'd in outward Appearance to be against the Rules of Religion, at least of common Piety and Conscience. In short, without this Consideration there could never have been so many Leagues broken as we find in *Guicciardine*: *Charles* the *Fifth* would never have abandoned the *Venetians* to the *Turks*: *Charles* the *Eighth* would not so easily have been driven out of *Italy: Paul* the *Fifth* would not so quietly have got Possession of the Dutchy of *Ferrara*, nor could the present Pope have seiz'd upon that of *Urbin:* So many Princes would not desire the Restitution of the *Palatinate*, nor the Prosperity of the King of *Sweden*, nor that *Casal* should remain to the Duke of *Mantua*, were it not by virtue of this Maxim, to set bounds to the unmeasurable Ambition of certain Nations who would put that in practice towards their neighbouring Princes, which rich Citizens do to the poor ones

> ——*O si angulus ille*
> *Parvulus accedat qui nunc denormat Agellum.*
> Hor. Book 2.

> Might that small Angle happen to my share
> 'Twould make this Field of mine so regular!

We might add, that the Law of Arms does not permit those People to be ill treated, who have surrender'd themselves, and implor'd the Mercy of their Conqueror, and yet when the number of Prisoners is so great that they cannot easily be guarded, provided for, or pinto a Place of Safety, or that their own Side will not Ransom them, it is allow'd by these Maxims to put them all to the Sword, since otherwise they might starve an Army, put them to defiance, favour the Enterprizes of their Companions, and cause a thousand other Difficulties. And for this Reason *Aldus Manutius*, Discourse III. has held, that *Hannibal* might be justly excus'd for slaying in the Temple of *Juno* all the *Roman* Captives that would not follow him when he left *Italy:*

although for this and some other Actions *Valerius Maximus* has given him this Character, *Hannibal cujus majori ex parte virtus sævitia constabat*, The Valour of *Hannibal* consisted most in Cruelty.

To such Maxims as these we may refer the manner of Acting, or particular Customs of certain Nations as to their own Government: As for Example, that of our *Salick* Law, so religiously observ'd touching the Succession of Males to the Crown, and the Exclusion of Females, by which Means the Crown was preserv'd from the Invasion of the *Spaniards* during the time of the League: The true and loyal *Frenchmen* having protested against all foreign Pretensions as null and void, and dismissed all the Rivals by this formal Text of the Law, *Francorum Regni successor Masculus esto*, Let the Successor to the Kingdom of the *Franks* be a Male.

The Law of the *Chinese* is much of the same Nature, which prohibits Strangers from coming into their Kingdom under pain of Death; That of the grand *Turk* to strangle all his Relations; that of the King of *Ormus* to put out their Eyes; that of the *Abyssins* to make them dwell upon the top of an inaccessible Mountain; the *Ostracisme* amongst the *Athenians*; the *Matze* to the *Valaix*, a People of *Germany*; the Council of *Discoli* at *Lucca*; the Lake *Orfano* at *Venice*; the Inquisition in *Spain* and *Italy*; and several other Laws and Customs peculiar to each Nation, which have no other Foundation of Right but these Reasons of State, and yet are all very religiously observ'd, as being necessary for the Conservation of those States that make use of them.

To conclude: The last thing that is to be consider'd in Politicks are these *master strokes* which may come under the same definition that we have already given to the *Maxims* and *Reasons of State*, *Ut sint excessus juris communis propter commune bonum*, or to explain it better, *Bold and extraordinary Actions, which Princes are constrain'd to execute when their Affairs are difficult and almost to be despair'd of, contrary to the common Right, without observing any Order or Form of Justice, but hazarding particular Interest for the good of the Publick.* But the better to distinguish between these Maxims, this may be added, that generally when any thing is done *Maxims*, all Causes, Reasons, Manifesto's, Declarations, and Forms and Methods to prove an Action lawful precede the Effects and Operations of them; whereas on the contrary, in these *master strokes of State*, the Thunderbolt falls before the Noise of it is heard in the Skies, *Ante ferit, quam flamma micet*, Prayers are said before the Bell is rung for them; the Execution precedes the Sentence; he receives the Blow that thinks he himself is giving it; he suffers who never expected it, and he dies that look'd upon himself to be the most secure; all is done in the Night and Obscurity, amongst Storms and Confusion, the Goddess *Laverna* presides, and the first Grace requested of her is this,

> *Da fallere, da sanctum justumque videre*
> *Noctem peccatis, & fraudibus objice Nubem.*

> Make me a Saint and Just to human Sight,
> But wrap my Cheats in Clouds, and Crimes in Night.

They have however so much that is good in them, that they have the same Justice and Equity that we said before lay under the *Maxims and Reasons of State*, but those Maxims might be publish'd before the Stroke, whereas the principal Rule observ'd in these, is to keep them conceal'd till they are finish'd. Of this sort were the remarkable Executions of the Count of St. *Paul* under *Lewis* the *Eleventh*, of the Marshal *de Biron* under *Henry* the *Fourth*, the Earl of *Essex* under *Elizabeth* Queen of *England*, the Marquis *D'Ancre* under the King now reigning; the two Brothers under *Henry* the *Third,* of *Majon* under *William* the *First,* King of *Sicily*, of *David Riccio* under *Mary* Queen of *Scots*, of *Spurius Melius* the *Roman* Knight under *Abala Servilius* Commander of the Horse; of *Sejanus* and *Plautian* under two several Emperors, which were all as lawful and necessary one as the other, and yet the three first ought to be refer'd to *Maxims* and *Reasons of State*, because the Process was made and Forms of Laws observ'd before their Execution, and all the rest to the *master strokes* of *State* and Refin'd Politicks, because no Proceedings were against them till their Execution. We may likewise bring this distinction, that although may Formalities might precede the execution of a Design, yet if Religion is mightily profan'd by it, as when the *Venetian* said, *Somo Venetiani, dopo Christiani, We are* Venetians *and afterwards Christians:* When a Christian Prince calls in the *Turk* to his Assistance; when *Henry* the *Eighth* made his Country revolt from the Holy See; when the Duke of *Saxony* encourag'd the Heresy of *Luther*; when *Charles* of *Bourbon* took *Rome*, imprison'd the Pope, and put three Cardinals to Death; or when the Affair is altogether extraordinary and of very great Consequence for the Good or Ill that may happen from it; then we may use this Term of a *master Stroke of State*, as we may judge by the following enumeration of some of them which have been put in Practice not by *Turks, Infidels* or *Cannibals*, but by Christian Princes, such as not to flatter or spare our own Nation have been Kings of *France*; amongst whom *Clovis* the first Christian King, committed some so strange and so far from all Justice, that I cannot imagine what thoughts that good Man *Savaron* must have when he wrote a Book of his Sanctity: *Charles* the *Seventh* made no scruple of carrying on his designs by *Joan* the Maid of *Orleans*; *Lewis* the *Eleventh* broke his Words given to the Constable, deceiv'd every one under the Veil of Religion, and made use of the *Hermite* the *Prevost* to put many Persons to death without any formal Proceedings; *Francis* the *First* was the Cause of the *Turks* coming into *Italy*, and would not observe the Treaty made at *Madrid*; *Charles* the *Ninth* consented to the memorable Massacre of St. *Bartholomew*, and to the secret Assassination of *Lignerolles* and *Bussy*; *Henry* the *Third* dispatch'd the *Guises*; *Henry* the *Fourth* made a League Offensive and Defensive with the *Hollanders*, not to mention his Conversion to the Catholick Religion; and *Lewis* the *Just*, all whose Actions were esteem'd Miracles, and his master strokes of State to be the effects of his Justice, practis'd two signal ones in the Death of the Marquis *D'Ancre*, and the Succours he sent to the *Valtoline*. As for the *Venetians*, if it is true that they hold constant to the Maxims abovemention'd, it must be confess'd that they remain plung'd in the depth of a continual *Matchiavelism*, not to mention several other things that they daily practice. The *Florentines* in rejoycing at the Captivity of St. *Lewis* in the *Holy Land*, did not so much make use of a *Secret* of *State*, as of an Action very discommendable and shameful: *It was remarkable*, says *Villani, that when the News came to* Florence *where the* Gibellins *were then in Power, they made a Feast in their great Hall.* Amongst the Popes we may take notice of the Prison of *Celestine*, the Poison of *Alexander* the *Sixth*, the Assassination of Father *Paul*, which was design't, though not perfected; which are two certain proofs, that they do not cease to be Men when they are elected to be Popes. *Charles* of *Anjou* King of *Sicily*, cut off the Heads of *Conradin* and *Frederick* of *Austria: Peter* of *Arragon* gave Authority to the *Sicilian* Vespers. *Alphonso* King of *Naples*, and *Alexander* the *Sixth* had recourse to *Bajazet* against the Forces of *Charles* the *Eighth* of *France*. The Emperor *Charles* the *Fifth*, did not give the Investiture of the Dutchy of *Milan* to the Duke of *Orleance*, though in his Passage through *France* he had promis'd to do it. The same Emperor just at the Time when he had it in his Power to Ruine the Protestants, rather chose to make use of them to invade *France*, and call'd them his *Black Guards*. He diverted that Money which *Germany* had contributed to the War against the *Turks*, to the Ruin of *Francis* the *First:* His Hatred to the King of *England* because of the Divorce from his Aunt, made *Rome* so violent against *Henry* the *Eighth*, and by this means gave occasion to the Change of Religion which then happen'd. After this he made a League with that King, and got him to take Arms against *France:* His General *Charles de Bourbon* took *Rome* and rais'd such a Persecution against the Ecclesiasticks, *that* (as it is in that Dialogue of *Charonte*) *no Man durst appear abroad in the Habit of a Fryar or a Priest.*

In short, in his time and by his Command, there was so great a Butchery of Men in the *Indies*, which were then newly discover'd, that it is beyond any credibility. *Philip* the *Second* would never suffer the Pope to meddle with the Affairs of *Portugal*, and hang'd up all the *French* Soldiers that were going to the Assistance of *Don Antonio*. And whoever does not know how much he labour'd for the Reconciliation of *Henry* the *Fourth* to the Church of *Rome*, may learn it from Cardinal *D'Ossat*'s Letters, where all those Artifices are recorded which at that time were practis'd against the *French* Monarchy. Now these Examples drawn only from the Histories of ten or twelve Princes being so many in Number, I am of Opinion that they may serve for an undoubted Proof to demonstrate, that though the Writings of *Matchiavel* are prohibited, his Doctrine has nevertheless been practis'd by the same Persons, whose Authority has censur'd them.

But having fully discours'd of the Definition, it is likewise necessary to consider, what the Division may be; the first and most natural way seems to be to divide them into just and injust, that is to say, into Monarchical, and Tyrannical; and that under the first we may place the death of *Plautian, Sejanus,* and the Marquis *D'Ancre*; and to the second that of *Remus* and *Conradin*.

Besides this Division, which I look upon as the principal, they may likewise be divided into such as regard the publick good, and others that have respect only to the private Interest of the People who undertake them. The first comprehends such Actions as that of *Hannibal*, who put to death a *Roman* Prisoner, who was in his Presence had slain an Elephant. *Dicens indignum vita qui cogi potuerat cum bestiis decertare;* Saying he was not fit to live, who was so mean as to be compell'd to fight with Beasts. Although it is much more probable as *Sarisburgensis* has judiciously observ'd (*Polycrat.* Book I. c. 2) *Eum noluisse Captivum inauditi triumphi gloria illustrari, & infamari Bestias quarum virtute terrorem Orbi incusserat;* He would not suffer a Captive to be honored with the Glory of an unheard of Triumph, and those Beasts should fall into any discredit, by whose Strength we had struck Terror through the Universe. So the People of *Elis* in *Greece* having brought *Phidias* the Statuary from *Athens* to make the Image of *Jupiter Olympius*, when he had perform'd his Work to admiration, thinking that if they let him return to *Athens* he might make another that might surpass it, accus'd him of Sacrilege and having cut off both his Hands, sent him home in that condition; *Nec puduit illos Jovem debere sacrilegio,* nor were they asham'd to owe their *Jupiter* to a Sacrilege, says *Seneca,* and the poor *Phidias, Talem fecit Jovem ut hoc ejus opus Elii ultimum esse vellent,* Made such a *Jove* as was to be the last Work he was to finish. As to those which regard a private Interest they have been practis'd by all the Legislators and New Prophets that we shall speak of hereafter.

They may likewise be divided into those which are fortuitous or casual; as when *Columbus* persuaded some of the Inhabitants of the new World, that he would take away the Moon from them (which was soon after to suffer an Eclipse) if they did not furnish him with plenty of

Provisions; and into those which were premeditated and undertaken upon a mature deliberation from the apparent Good that they judge may proceed from them, as most of those were which we have lately discours'd of.

There are likewise some that are single or determin'd by one blow, as the Death of *Sejanus*, and some that are compounded, that is, follow'd or preceded by several others; preceded, as that of St. *Bartholomew* by the death of *Lignerolles*, the Marriage of the King of *Navarre*, and the wounding of the Admiral; follow'd, as the Execution of the Marquis of *Ancre* by that of *Travail*, of his Wife the *Marchioness*, and the Exile of the *Queen-Mother*.

There are some which are done by Princes, when the Necessity and Conjuncture of their Affairs require them, of which only we shall treat in this Discourse; and others which are executed by their Ministers, making use of their Master's Authority to accomplish many things, either for their own private Interest, or that of the Publick, without letting the Prince know the first Springs and Motions, so we see the advancement of *Postell*, under *Francis* the first, was a Trick of State of the *Chancellor Poyet*, that the ill Character of *Bigot* the Philosopher given to the same King was another, done by *Castellan* Bishop of *Mascon*: And in our times, the Death of *Reboul*, the Imprisonment of the Abbot *du Bois*, and the giving of the Cardinal's That to Monsieur *d'Ossat*, were attributed to Monsieur *de Villeroy*, as *Perron*'s That was to Monsieur *de Sully*, and the Execution of *Travail* to Monsieur *de Luynes*. But because the more Divisions may be troublesome and superfluous, I shall content my self with these already set down, and proceed to the following Chapter.

CHAP. III. *With what Precautions, and upon what Occasions these Refin'd Politicks may be made use of.*

I Come now to what is most essential as to this Discourse, and since discreet and good Physicians, never order violent and dangerous Remedies, without directing what Precautions are necessary to make them truly useful, so I think it proper to do upon this Occasion, and shall be the more willing, because these *Master Strokes* of *State* are like a Sword, that may be manag'd well or ill, as the Launce of *Telehus* that can kill or cure; or like *Diana* at *Ephesus* that had two Faces, one sad, the other pleasant; in short, like the Medals invented by the Hereticks, which represent the Devil and the Pope under the same Features and Lineaments, or the Pictures that shew Death and Life, according to the different sides that you stand to look upon them: Besides, none but a *Timon* would set up Gibbets to let Men hang themselves upon them; and for my own part, I have too much regard for Nature, and that Humanity which she prescribes us, to relate those Histories, on purpose that People might take ill Examples from them.

Tam fœlix utinam quam pectore candidus essem,
Extat adhuc nemo faucius ore me.

Were I as happy, as my Breast is free

Therefore being about to lay down the Rules which ought to be observed, that Honour, Justice, Profit and Decency may be preserv'd, I shall have recourse to those which *Charon* has given in his third Book, Chap. 2. and I shall place that first which is upon the defensive, and not the offensive, to preserve, and not to make ones self great, but to fence off Surprize, Deceits and Villanies, rather than to commit them: The World is full of Artifice and Malice, *per fraudem & dolum regna evertuntur*, by Fraud and Treachery Kingdoms are subverted, says *Aristotle*; *Tu servari per eadem nefas esse vis,* and would you think it Wickedness to preserve them by the same Methods? says *Lipsius.* It is permitted to counterplot what is plotted against us, and to play the *Fox* with an old *Reynard:* The Laws pardon such Faults as Force obliges us to commit, *Insitum est unicuique animali*, says Salust, *ut se vitamque tueatur,* Self-preservation is a natural Instinct, and according to *Tully,* (Book 3. of his Offices) *Communis Utilitatis derelictio contra naturam est,* It is against Nature to fly from our own Security: It is therefore sometimes necessary to let the Byass run more than usually to one side, to accommodate our selves to Times and Persons, to mix Honey with the Gall, for by the Application of a Caustick only, nothing is effected, but to leave a Rancour behind it.

The second is, That it be done out of Necessity, for the evident and important Good of the State or Prince for whom it is designed; it is a necessary and indispensable Obligation, it is always a Duty to procure the Publick Good, *semper officio fungitur*, (says *Cicero* in the same place) *utilitati hominum consulens & Societati*, He is always doing his Duty, consulting for Society, and the Good of Mankind. This Law which is so common, and ought to be the principal Guide of all the Actions of Princes, *Salus Populi suprema Lex esto*, Let the Safety of the People be the Supreme Law, absolves them from abundance of the little Circumstances and Formalities to which Justice would oblige them, so they are Masters of the Laws to extend or mitigate, or confirm or abolish them, not as it may seem good to themselves, but as Reason and the Publick Safety requires: The Honour of the Prince, the Love of the Country, and the Welfare of the People, are an equivalent for some little Faults and Injustices; to which, not with a design to prophane any Passage of the Scriptures, may be applied to the Counsel of *Caiphas* the High-Priest to the *Jews, That it was expedient that one man should die for the People.*

The third is, rather to march slowly, than to drive furiously, seeing

> *Nulla unquam de morte Hominis cunctatio longa est.*

> In case of Death there's no Delay is long.
> *Claudian.*

And that it be not made an Art of Trade, least the frequent use should be attended with some Injustice. Experience teaches us, that all such things as are wonderful and extraordinary are not seen every Day, Comets don't appear but at the distance of some Ages, Monsters, Deluges, Eruptions of *Vesuvius*, and Earthquakes happen rarely, and this uncommoness of the Appearance gives a Lustre and Beauty to abundance of tings which suddenly lose it when they become too frequent.

> *Vilia sunt nobis quæcunque prioribus annis*
> *Vidimus; & sordet quicquid spectavimus olim.*

> The Thing we often see but vile appears,
> And the Contempt increases with its Years.

I may add, that if a Prince keeps himself within these Bounds, he cannot well be blam'd, nor upon that account be reputed as a barbarous or perfidious Tyrant, since these Denominations are to be applied only to such as have contracted an habit of those ill Qualities and Habits depend upon a great number of Actions often repeated, *Habitus est Actus multoties repetitus*, as a Line is a Continuation of Points, and a Superficies a Multiplication of Lines.

The fourth Rule is, that choice be always made of such Methods as are most easie and gentle, and care be taken of that Maxim which *Claudian* gave to the Emperor *Honorius*,

> ——*Metii satiabere pœnis:*
> *Triste rigor nimius.*

> The Horror is too tragic for our Eyes,
> What *Metius* has endur'd, let that suffice.

It belongs only to Tyrants to say, *Sentiat se mori*, Let him feel that he is dying, and to Devils to be pleas'd with the Torments of Mankind: There shou'd not be any Resemblance with the Horses at the Olympick Race, which can never be curb'd when once upon their Carreer, the proceeding must be by a Judge, and not a Party; by a Physician, and not a Hangman; like a Man reserv'd, prudent, wise and discreet, and not as one that is cholerick, revengeful, and given up to all sorts of violent and extraordinary Passions: This Virtue of Clemency teaches us that

> *Quæ docet ut pœnis hominum vel sanguine pasci*
> *Turpe ferumque putes.*

> None but a fierce and brutish Mind,
> Feeds on the Blood and Torments of Mankind.

and is always more esteem'd than Rigour or Severity. The Club of *Hercules*, as the Poets say, was given him to vanquish Gyants, punish Tyrants, destroy Monsters, and yet it was made of an Olive Tree, as a Symbol of Peace and Tranquillity; it is possible to ease a great Tree that is dying, by lopping off some of the Branches, and letting Blood at a seasonable time, often prevents extraordinary Diseases: In short, this is to imitate a good Surgeon, who begins with Operations, that may be easily supported; and even the *Jews* gave certain Liquors to drink to condemn'd Persons, to take away the Sense and Pain of their Sufferings; the Head of *Sejanus* might have satisfy'd *Tiberius*; *Hannibal* might have made his Captives unserviceable, without killing them, and the sacking of *Rome* might have been less odious, if there had been more regard shewn to the Churches and their Priests, and the Marquis *d'Ancre* had not been less justly punish'd, though he had not been dragg'd along and torn to pieces. *Illos crudeles vocabo* (says *Seneca* in his third Book of Clemency) *qui puniendi causam habent, modum non habent*; They may be call'd cruel who have reason to punish, but don't carry a Mien or Temper in the doing of it.

The fifth is, That to justifie these Actions, and diminish the blame that is generally cast upon them, when Princes find themselves reduc'd to the necessity of practising them, they should do it with Concern and Regret, as a Father that suffers the Limb of his Child to be cut off to save its Life, or as Persons draw a Tooth to gain some Rest, it is what the Poet does not forget in his Description of a good Prince;

> *Sit piger ad pænas Pinceps, ad præmia velox.*
> *Quique dolet quoties cogitur esse ferox.*

> —He's slow to punish, eager to reward,
> And grieves when forc'd to do a thing that's hard.

therefore such sort of Operations ought to be retarded, rather than hasten'd too much, to be often revolv'd in the Mind, and all things are to be thought of to avoid them if possible, and should be done with the same Reluctancy, as a Man in a Tempest at Sea, would sacrifice all his Goods to the Fury of that Element.

It is not my Intention to conclude the number of these Rules, by any one that shou'd be thought to be the last that is worthy of Observation, for I do not judge it fitting to prescribe limits to Clemency and Humanity, let them extend their Bounds as far as they can, they shall always seem to me to be too much strained. When there is no Fear that the Horse should stumble, we may give him the loose Rein, when the Wind is fair we may hoist all the Sails, Virtues can be endanger'd by nothing but contrary Vices, and whilst they are at a sufficient distance from them, there is no need to restrain them: It is very true that they have not to free a Carreer in the Subject we are treating of, as in several others, but this will be sufficient, that a Prince who cannot be altogether good, may be partly so; and he that for a superior Reason cannot be altogether good, may be partly so; and he that for a superior Reason cannot be just, may not be altogether cruel, unjust, and wicked; but though we had only these five Rules and Precautions, in my Opinion these are sufficient to let any one that has the least Inclination to do good, see what is Reason, and though I had not set them down so distinctly, yet Discretion and his own Judgment, would not let a prudent Man be ignorant of them. Seeing

Quid faciat, quid non homini Prudentia monstrat. (Palingenius.)

It is likewise my Intention, that all the Histories I have, or shall hereafter relate, may only so far pass for justifiable, as they may be found conformable to right Reason, when they are applied to these five Rules or to those of general Prudence.

But all the forementioned Maxims and Precautions serving only to render us only better instructed and disposed for the Execution of the Master Strokes of State; we now see in what Rencounters and upon what Occasions the are to be practis'd, *Charon* in *Book of Wisdom* (*Book 3. c. 2.*) without seeming to design it, proposes three or four, but it is briefly *a la Sfugita*, as the *scythians* let fly their surest Arrows when they seem to be flying fastest. I shall extend them farther by Reasons and Examples and add several others which will serve as Heads or Titles to which these that are found in Historians and other Authors may be referr'd.

Now upon these Occasions there is no doubt but they should be plac'd first tho' perhaps they may be the most unjust which happen upon the new Erection and Establishment, or the change of Principalities and Kingdoms: And first to speak of new Erections, if we consider the Beginning of all Monarchies we shall find they have had their Rise from such Inventions and by Deceits, by making Religion and Miracles march at the Head of a long Train of Barbarities and Cruelties, *Titus Livius* (Book 4. Decad. I.) was the first that made this Remark: *Datur hæc Venia Antiquitati, ut miscendo Humana divinis, primordia urbium augustiora faciat*; We must give this Allowance to Antiquity that by mingling Divine things with humane we may render the Foundation of Cities more solemn; which hereafter we shall shew to be very true, but at present, we shall mention nothing but what is general and begin our

Proof by the Establishments of the four first and greatest Monarchies of the World. The so much renowned *Semiramis*, who founded the Empire of the *Assyrians* took great Pains to persuade her People, that being expos'd in her Infancy, the Birds were so careful as to nourish her, and bring her Food in their Bills as they do to their young ones, and being desirous to confirm this Fable by the last Action of her Life, order'd that a Report should be spread, after her Decease, that she was turn'd into a Dove, and that she flew away with a great many other Birds, that came into her Chamber to attend her: She had likewise Resolution enough to counterfeit the changing of her Sex, and to represent the Person of her Son *Ninus*, and to imitate him in all his Actions, and the better to succeed in this Enterprise, she introduced a new sort of Habit amongst the People, which might most easily hide every thing that should discover her to be a Woman, *Brachia enim ac crura velamentis, caput Tiara tegit, & ne novo habitu aliquid occultare videretur eodem ornatu populum vestiri jubet, quem morem vestis exinde gens universa tenet,* For her Garments cover'd her Arms and Legs, and she had a Tiara upon her Head, and lest there might seem as if something was conceal'd under this new Habit, she commanded all her Subjects to wear the same, which Fashion has ever since continued in the Nation; and by this means, *primis initiis sexum mentita, puer credita est.* Having from the beginning dissembled her Sex, she was thought to be a Boy, (*Justin* Book I.) *Cyrus* who established the Monarchy of the *Persians*, would add to his Authority, by that Vine which his Grandfather *Astyages* saw springing, *Ex naturalibus filiæ cujus palmite omnis* Asia *obumbrabatur,* from his Daughter and overshadowing all *Asia*. And by the Dream he had that he should take Arms and chuse a Slave for his Companion in all his Enterprises; besides this, he raised an opinion, that a Bitch had given him suck, in a Wood, where he had been exposed by *Harpagus*, till such time as a Shepherd finding him by chance carried him home to his Wife and bred him up carefully in his Cottage. As for *Alexander* and *Romulus* as their Designs had a farther Reach, so it was necessary to practise more prevailing Stratagems; for which reason, though they as well as the former, began by that of their Birth, et they carried it as high as it was possible, from which *Sidonius* took occasion to say:

> Magnus Alexander *nec non* Romanus *habentur*
> *Concepti serpente Deo.*

> The *Alexanders* both of *Greece* and *Rome*
> Were got by Gods in Serpents Shapes conceal'd.

As for Alexander, he made People believe that *Jupiter* was us'd to converse with his Mother *Olympias*, and that when he came into the World, the Goddess *Diana* was so diligent in her Assistance at his Mother's Labour, that she never thought of preserving her own Temple at *Ephesus*, which, in the mean time, was entirely consum'd, by an accidental Fire. That he might farther establish this Opinion of his Divinity amongst his Subjects, he so disposed the Priests of *Jupiter Ammon* in *Ægypt, ut ingredientem Templum statim ut* Ammonis *filium salutarent*, that they should instantly salute him as the Son of *Ammon*, (*Justin* 1. II.) And that he might the better act his part, *Regat num omnes patris interfectores fit ultus, respondent patrem ejus nec posse interfici nec mori,* He asks whether he had reveng'd himself upon all his Father's Murtherers, they answered him that his Father could neither be murder'd or die: He soon after shew'd the Effects of this Contrivance; for he commanded *Parmenio* to destroy all the Temples and abolish all the Honours which the Eastern People render'd to *Jason, Ne cujusquam Nomen in Oriente Venerabilius quam* Alexandri *esset,* That there might be no name in the East, more venerable than that of *Alexander.* To this may be added, that when some Captives had discovered to him a Remedy against the poison'd Arrows of the *Indians,* before he made it publick, he told the People that it was reveal'd to him in a Dream. But this insatiable Ambition having carried him so far as to make himself ador'd, he found himself at last, by the Remonstrances of *Callisthenes,* the Obstinacy of the *Lacedæmonians,* and the Wounds he received in the Wars, that all his management was not sufficient to confirm this new Apotheosis; and that there was need of more good Fortune to gain an inferior Place in Heaven than to conquer here below and Domineer over the whole Word. If to these Histories we add that of the Death of his Father *Philip,* to which he and his Mother *Olympias* consented, as likewise that of *Clytus,* whom he slew, with his own Hand, because he had got too much Authority amongst the Soldiers, we shall find that *Alexander* practis'd that in Secret, which *Cæsar* afterwards did more openly, *Si violandum est jus, regnandi causa,* If Law is to be violated, it is for the sake of Empire. As to *Romulus* he rais'd a Reputation by the Story of the God *Mars,* his having Conversation with his Mother

Rhea, by that of the Wolf which nourished him, the Death of his Brother, the Asylum which he established at *Rome*, the Rape of the *Sabines*, the Murther of *Tatius* which he suffered to go unpunish'd, and lastly his Death, by drowning himself in the Marshes to make his People believe that his Body was taken up into Heaven, because it could not be found upon Earth. Now if to the *Master Stroaks* of *Romulus*, we add those which *Numa Pompilius* practis'd by the Intervention of the Nymph *Egeria*, and the superstitious Rites that he instituted during his Reign, it will afterwards be easie to judge, by what means *Rome* came to its Grandeur.

> *Quibus auspiciis illa inclyta* Roma
> *Imperium terris, animos æquavit Olympo.*
> Virgil.

> *Rome* whose Ascending Tow'rs shall Heaven invade.
> Involving Earth and Ocean in her Shade,
> High as the Mother of the Gods in Place,
> And proud, like her, of an Immortal Race.
> Mr. *Dryden*.

It is likewise not improper to remark, that as the Monarchical Government could not be founded without so many Tricks and so much Cunning, yet there were as many necessary to cause its Ruin, when the *Tarquins* being driven from *Rome* for the Rape of *Lucrece*, the Monarchy was changed into a Republick. For we may first observe the dissembled Madness of *Junius Brutus*, his pretended Fall, the Execution of his two Sons, as well because they were Friends to the *Tarquins* and accus'd of having a Design of Bringing them back to the City, as because the Education they had received, during the Monarchy, was directly contrary to that he was going about to settle; and to finish all these Actions by a *Master Stroke* of State, and by a true *Arcanum Imperii*; He banish'd *Tarquinius Collatinus* from *Rome*, though he had been the Husband of *Lucretia*, his Colleague in the Consulship, and had contributed as much as he had done to the Expulsion of the *Tarquins:* for tho' he made it his Pretext that the name of the *Tarquins* was become so odious to the *Romans* that they could not bear it even in the Person of their Friends: Yet his principal Aim was not to let any one of those remain who had push'd Matters to the last Extremity, and that he might not divide the Glory of that Action with one whose Merit he had publickly confess'd, *Meminimus, fatemur, ejecisti Reges, absolve beneficium tuum, aufer hinc regium nomen,* (Livy *Book* 2.) It must be confess'd we remember that you expell'd the Kings, complete your Benefit, and carry hence the very name of them.

And if we would examine all the other Monarchies and Estates, that are inferior to these four, we may find History enough of this kind to fill a large Volume, therefore it shall suffice for the last Proof of this Maxim to consider that *Mahomet* practis'd to establish his Religion, together with that Empire which is the greatest in the World at present. Indeed as all Persons of great Spirits have been careful to take advantage of the most signal Disgraces that have happen'd to them, so he likewise did the same, for perceiving himself very subject to the falling Sickness, he made his Friends believe that the most violent *Fits* of his *Epilepsy* were so many Extasies and Signs of the Spirit of God, that descended upon him, he persuaded them likewise that a white Pigeon, that he had taught to eat Corn out of his Ear, was the Angel *Gabriel*, who came from God to tell him what he was to do; after this he made use of one *Sergius* a Monk, to compose an *Alcoran*, which they feigned to be dictated by God himself, and at last he got a famous Astrologer to dispose the People by his Predictions, that a change should happen in the State, and a new Law should be given them by a great Prophet, to receive that more easily which he was about to publish: But one time perceiving that his Secretary *Abdala Bensalon*, against whom he had taken a Disgust, without any Reason, began to discover and talk of his Impostures, he cut his Throat in the night time, in his own house, and set Fire to the four corners of it, and the next day persuaded the People that this Fire was sent from Heaven as a Punishment to him for corrupting some Passages of the *Alcoran*. But this was not the last of his Contrivances, he had one *Master Piece* to finish withal; He persuaded one of his most faithful Domesticks to go down to the bottom of a Well, that was near the highway, and as he was passing by with a great Multitude following him, as there was usually, to cry out, *Mahomet is the beloved of God, Mahomet is the beloved of God:* This being done in the manner that was proposed, he immediately return'd Thanks to the divine Goodness for so signal a Testimony, and desir'd all the People that attended him immediately to fill up this Well and build a little Mosque upon it for the Memorial of such a Miracle. And by this Invention the poor Servant was soon knocked on the Head, and buried under a Heap of Stones, that hinder'd him from ever discovering this Miracle, But,

> *Excepit sed Terra sonum, calamique loquaces,*

> The Earth and whistling Reeds receiv'd the Sound.
> *Petronius* Epig.

The second Occasion that there may be of practising these subtle Contrivances, is the Preservation or Reestablishment of States and Principalities, when by some Misfortune, or length of time, which diminishes and consumes every thing, they begin to tend to ruin and threaten a sudden Downfal unless Care be taken to preserve them. And indeed seeing all things desire their own Preservation, and are oblig'd, as much as 'tis possible, to maintain the Principles of their Being and their Safety; I am persuaded, that it is allowed nay even necessary that that should serve for their Support, which ser'vd at first for their Establishment: I may add that if the Opinion of *Ovid* be true,

> *Non minor est virtus quam quærere, para tueri,*
> *Casus inest illic, hic erit Artis opus.*

> 'Tis no less Virtue to preserve than gain,
> This is the Work of Chance but that of Art.

it is reasonable to conclude that these refin'd Politicks may be more justly made use of for the Defence than the raising of a Monarchy; for before a State or Government was fram'd, there was no Necessity for the establishment of it, seeing such things have often proceeded from Chance, or been the effect of the Power or Ambition of some particular Person: But on the contrary, when it is once settled it ought afterwards to be maintain'd.

Now not to be like these Vagabonds or Gipsies

Quos aliena juvant propriis habitare molestum est,

Who have no Home but dwell at others Costs.

It will not be improper, after having recounted these Examples, to turn over our own History, since it contains those which are as remarkable as the *Greek* or *Roman*. And indeed when I consider what was done by *Clovis* our first Christian King, I must confess that I never saw any thing that came up to it in all Antiquity; for the Country of the *Gauls* was then divided into four different Nations, of which the *Visigoth* possessed *Gascony*, the *Burgundian* was Master of the *Lionnois*, the *Roman* commanded in *Soissons* and the neighbouring Provinces, and the *Franks* who were then almost all Pagans, govern'd the remainder: He was desirous to unite and bring together these four divided parts under his own Dominion, as *Æsculapius* did to the Limbs of *Hippolytus*. To accomplish this Design, perceiving that Paganism began insensibly to lose ground and become antiquated, after having gain'd the Battle of *Tolbiac* over a *German* Prince, he took the Resolution to become a Christian, and by that means please *Clotilda* the Queen, a great number of Prelates and all the common People of *France*. Upon which I may make this Remark, that although it would be more decent to attribute these first Motives of so considerable a Change to some holy Inspiration obtain'd by the Prayers of the good Queen *Clotilda*, and that I should interprete every thing that is doubtful in the best sense; yet in this place I may rank my self amongst the Politicians, who are the only People that have the Privilege of interpreting things otherwise, or at least of finding out some Craft or Stratagem in them, that there may always appear to be something in them that is refin'd, to quicken the Spirits of such Persons as they instruct, by the recital of such remarkable Actions, and passing a Judgment upon them as if they were true, though they are often founded upon Conjectures and Suspicions, which can in no wise be prejudicial to the Truth of History. Let us proceed therefore to speak of this Conversion of *Clovis*, according to the Sentiments of *Pasquier* and some other Politicians: We shall say, that the sacred Oil and the Auriflamb or Banner, of which *Paulus Æmilius* makes no mention, were so many Contrivances of State to give Authority to the change of his Religion, which he would make use of as a powerful Machine to ruine all his little neighbouring Princes. And in truth he began with the *Romans* who had incurr'd the common Hatred of all foreign Nations, then he encounters the *Visigoths*, upon Pretence that they were *Arians*, and at last he fell upon the Princes *Regnacaire, Cacarie, Sigebert,* and his Son descendants of *Clodion*, who had taken Possession of some small scantlings of *France*, and caus'd them all to be treacherously assassinated, without any other pretext, than to avoid the Resentment they might one

Day have of the Wrong *Meroveus* his Grandfather had done them. After this any one may judge (as I have hinted before) what reason Monsieur *Savaron* could have to endeavour to prove, that *Clovis* was a Saint. In my opinion, the best proof which can be given us is to make him say, as a certain Poet did *Scipio*,

> *Si fas cædendo cœlestia scandere regna*
> *Mi soli cæli maxima porta patent.*

> If we by Slaughter to the Heav'ns may fly
> To me the largest Gate does open lie.

But as the Wisdom of Men is Foolishness with God, it happen'd that his Successors suffering themselves to be led by the Nose by the *Masters* of the *Palace*, the Kingdom at last, after the change of divers Hands, came to *Pepin* an off-set of the Family of *Clodion*, as *Pasquier* has shown it, and so contributed to the good of the true Line, and united the Kingdom of *France*, but could not long preserve it in his own Family or its Descendants.

France being so reunited by *Clovis*, and afterwards much augmented by *Charlemagne*, continu'd a long time in a flourishing Condition till the *English* made a War upon it, which they pursued to obstinately, that being almost become Masters of it, it was necessary under *Charles* the *Seventh*, to have recourse to some refin'd Stroke to drive them thence; which was to that of *Joan* the Maid of *Orleans*, which is confess'd to be such a piece of Policy by *Justus Lipsius* in his Politicks, and some other Historians; but particularly by two of our own, that is, *Bellay Langey* in his Art of War, and *Haillot* in his History, not to mention several other less considerable Authors. Now this having succeeded so happily, and she being only burnt in Effigie, our Affairs began a little while after to grow worse, as well by means of the preceding Wars as of those that follow'd. *France* was like unsound Bodies, full of ill Humours and Pthisick, that cannot breathe but by Art, and are sustain'd only by the help of Remedies. For after that time she was not supported but by the Stratagems of *Lewis* the *Eleventh*, *Francis* the *First*, and *Charles* the *Ninth*, and others of our Princes, some of which shall be mention'd hereafter, as I find occasion.

The third Reason which may authorize these refin'd Politicks is, when the business is to lessen or abolish some Rights, Privileges, Franchises, and Exemptions which the Subjects enjoy to the Prejudice and Diminution of the Power of the Prince. So when *Charles* the *Fifth* would ruine the Right of Election, and secure the Empire in his own Family, he to that end made use of the Preaching of *Luther*, and gave him time enough to establish his Tenets, that so his Doctrine taking foot in *Germany*, a Division might spring up amongst the Electors, and that he might more easily ruine them, when it was a proper time to undertake it. It is what has been so judiciously remark'd by Monsieur *de Nevers*, in his Discourse printed in the Year 1590. upon the Posture of Affairs of State, dedicated to Pope *Sixtus* the *Fifth*, the Passage is this:

The pretence of Religion (says he) is no new thing, and many great Princes have made use of it to attain their Ends. I shall only mention the War which *Charles* the *Fifth* made against the Protestant Princes, for he would never have undertaken it if it had not been with an intention to make the Imperial Crown become Hereditary to the House of *Austria*, therefore he attack'd the ELectoral Princes to ruine and abolish this Election: For if Zeal for the Honour of God and the desire of maintaining the holy Catholick Religion, had been predominant in his Mind, he would never have staid from the Year 1519, when he was elected Emperor, till the Year 1549, before he took Arms, since the Heresy of *Luther*, which began to kindle in *Germany* about the Year 1526, might have then been easily extinguish'd without setting on Fire so great a part of *Europe*. But because he thought this Novelty might bring him greater Benefit than Damage, both in regard to the Pope and the Princes of *Germany*, because of the Division that would be occasion'd amongst them; not only between the secular Princes and the others, but even amongst the meanest Laicks: he suffer'd it to increase till it produc'd the Effect that he had projected, and then he stirr'd up *Paul* the *Third* to make War against the Protestants, under the pretence of Religion; whereas it was in truth to extirpate them and make the Monarchy become Hereditary to his House.

This was likewise taken notice of by *Francis* the *First*, in his *Apology* made in the Year 1537. *The Emperor, under colour of Religion, strengthened by a Catholick League made amongst the Catholicks, would oppose the others and may way for his Monarchy.* It was in truth a very great design, with a long reach, and contriv'd with much Judgment and Prudence. But *Philip* the *Second* made use of another that had a more quicker and more certain Effect, though it were in an Affair of less Consequence, which was only the abolishing the Privileges that had been enjoy'd by the Kingdom of *Arragon*, which were so advantageous, and so vigorously maintain'd by that People, that the Kings of *Spain* could not boast of an absolute Command over them. A fair occasion presented it self for that purpose, *Antonio Perez* his Secretary, and their Countryman, after having broke Prison in *Castile*, was retir'd into *Arragon* to secure his Life by the Privileges of that Country: *Philip* thought he had now a fair Pretence to get such a Thorn out of his Foot; wherefore having underhand concerted it with the *Jesuits*, that they should excite the People to take Arms and defend the Privileges and Liberties of their Country, he therefore assembles a great Army and seems as if he would encounter the *Arragonians:* In the mean time he *Jesuits* begin to play their part, and sing another Song, remonstrating to the People, that the King had Reason on his side, that his Forces were too weak to stand the hazard of any Engagement, after which there would be no hopes of Pardon. In short, they manag'd the matter so well, that Fear and Consternation fell upon the *Arragonians,* their Army was dispers'd, every one was amaz'd, fled and hid himself. In the mean time the King's Army passes through the

Country, enters the City of *Saragossa*, builds a Cittadel, demolishes the principal Houses; some were executed, others banish'd, and nothing omitted that might entirely ruine and subdue that Province, which is now more subject to the absolute Will of the King of *Spain* than any other. On the contrary, when some extraordinary Law is to be establish'd, some Regulation of Consequence to be made, or some severe Judgment to be pass'd, it is necessary to use the same Means, and to have recourse to these Maxims: And of this we have some Examples amongst the *Romans* and other wise Nations, that we have no longer any room to doubt of it. Could any thing be more cruel than to decimate a whole Legion for the Cowardice of some particular Soldiers? And yet this Custom was strictly observ'd amongst the *Romans*, to keep the Soldiers in their Duty by the Terror of such Punishments. And the same *Romans* to hinder the Attempts which Slaves might make upon their Masters, order'd that when such a Crime had been committed in a Family, all the Slaves that belong'd to it should be slain at their Master's Funeral: And this Law was so religiously observ'd, that *Pedanius* the chief Officer of the City being murder'd by one of his Slaves, there were four hundred Executed notwithstanding the Intercession that all the People of *Rome* made for them, and even against the Opinion of several of the Senators, who were so vigorously oppos'd by *Cassius*, and with such forceable Reasons, that he carried the Point, though it was thought to be against the Laws of Humanity, as it is related by *Tacitus* in the fourth Book of his Annals. This is likewise the Precept of *Cicero* (in his first Book of Offices) That *ita probanda est mansuetudo atque Clementia ut Reipublicæ causa abhibeatur severitas, sine quâ administrari Civitas non potest*, Good Nature and Clemency are to be approv'd of in such a degree, as that Severity may be made use of in the Necessities of the Commonwealth, for without that no City can be govern'd. The *Persians* had anciently this Law to secure the Life of their Prince, that whoever attempted it was not only punish'd in his own Person, but in those of his whole Kindred, who were put to Death in the same manner, as is particularly remarkable in the Story of *Bessus.* And *Ferdinando Pinto* says, he had been in a Kingdom where the same Custom was put in practice upon fifty or sixty Persons, that were akin to a young Page, who at the Age of ten or twelve Years had been so bold as to stab his Prince. The great *Tamerlane* understanding that a Soldier in his Army had drank a Quart of Milk and refus'd to pay for it, order'd his Belly to be rip'd up in the Presence of all his Companions, that by so extraordinary an Example he might keep them in Obedience to his Commands. The Crimes of Coining false Money, and Heresy, were not more heinous a hundred Years ago than at present, and yet Coiners are now boil'd in Oil, and Hereticks burnt alive, for no other end but to strike Terror into the Minds of those People, who by the single Prohibition of their Prince, could not be kept within the Bounds of their Duty; *Et sic multorum saluti potius quam libidini consulendum*, And so the Safety of the Multitude is to be consulted rather than their Appetite, says *Salust.*

Another Occasion of remaining rigid in the execution of these Maxims, is, when it is necessary to ruine some Power, which being too great, numerous, or extensive, cannot easily be humbled by any other Methods.

>   ——*Cum illam*
> *Defendant numerus, junctæque umbone Phalanges.*

And though it was extremely to be wish'd that it might always be accomplish'd as easily as the Kings of *Spain* did that of banishing the *Moriscos* and *Marons* out of their Kingdoms, to the number of above two hundred and forty thousand Familes, and that by virtue of a single Edict: Nevertheless, because all Affairs are not alike in their Circumstances, nor Diseases attended by the same Symptoms, so it is necessary to change the Medicines often, to use some that are more violent than others.

> *Ulcera possesses alte suffusa medullis,*
> *Non leviore manu, ferro curantus & igne;*
> *Ad vivum penetrant flammæ, quo funditus humor*
> *Defluat, & vacuis corrupto sanguine venis*
> *Arescat fons ille mali.*   Claudian. 3. in

Eutrop.

> When Ulcers through th' venom'd Marrow flow,
> 'Tis no soft Hand, but unrelenting Blow,
> With Steel and Fire that must the Cure begin,
> Then to the quick the subtle Flame breaks in;
> Dries up the Spring of this corrupted Blood,
> And sends the Humours forth with an impetuous

Flood.

The Slaughter which *Mithridates* made in one Day of forty thousand Roman Citizens, dispers'd in several Provinces of *Asia*, was one of those Strokes of Policy of which I am speaking; so were likewise the *Sicilian Vespers*, authoriz'd by *Peter* King of *Aragon*, and subtly contriv'd by *Prochytus*, a great Lord of the Country, who under the Disguise of a *Cordelier*, form'd his Party so well, that upon *Easter-Day*, (or as some say *Pentecost*) in the Year 1282, when the Bell went for *Vespers*, the *Sicilians* should massacre all the *French* that were in their Islands, without sparing so much as Women or Children; such a Story happen'd about twenty Years ago in the *Isle of Magna*, where the Inhabitants of the City of *Corma* deliver'd themselves after the same manner, and in one Night, from an Army of thirty thousand Men, that had been sent thither by *Arcomat*, General of the King of *Persia*. But since we have in our *French* History the Example of St. *Bartholomew*, which is more signal than any that is to be found in any other: Let us consider it in all its principal Circumstances, It was undertaken by Queen *Katherine de Medicis* provok'd by the Death of Captain Monsieur *Charry*, by Monsieur *de Guise*, who would revenge the Assassination of his Father committed by *Poltrot* at the Instigation of the Admiral and the Protestants, and by King *Charles*, and the Duke of *Anjou*, the first desiring a Satisfaction for the Retreat which the Protestants forc'd him to make sooner than he would have done from *Meaux* to *Paris*, and both thinking to ruin the *Hugunots*, who had been the cause of all those Troubles and Massacres which had happen'd for the space of thirty or forty Years in that Kingdom. The Affair had been concerted for many Years, and with such a resolution to keep it secret, that *Lignerolles*, Gentleman to the Duke of *Anjoy*, having signified to the King, though with the utmost Privacy that he knew something of it, he was dispatch'd immediately in a Duel, that the King underhand occasion'd him to be engag'd in. *Paris* was the place chose out to assemble, the People of the best Rank and Quality among the *Huguenots*; the reason for it was the Solemnity of the Marriage between *Henry* of *Navarre*, who was of that Religion, and Queen *Margaret*; the Wound given by the Duke of *Guise* to his old Enemy the Admiral, was the beginning of the Tragedy; the manner of executing it was by causing twelve hundred Carbineers, and the Companies of *Swiss* to march to *Paris*, was approv'd of by the Admiral, as believing it was to defend him against the House of *Lorrain*; in short, all was so well dispos'd, that nothing fail'd but in the Execution, in which, if they had proceeded with Rigour, it must have been confess'd that it had been the most daring Stroke, and carry'd on with the most refin'd Policy that had ever appear'd, either in *France* or any other places. As for my self, although St. *Bartholomew* be at present equally condemn'd by Protestants and Catholicks, and though *Thuanus* has deliver'd his Father's Opinion and his own, by these Verses of *Statius*.

> *Occidat illa dies ævo, neu postera credant*
> *Sæcula, nos certe taceamus & obtruta multa*
> *Nocte, tegi propriæ patiamur crimina gentis.*

> Let that Day in Times Annals ever die,
> Let us at least defend it from the Light,
> And hide our Nation's Crimes in dead of Night.

I shall not nevertheless fear to say, that it was a very just and very remarkable Action, and that the Cause was more than lawful, although the Effects were very dangerous and extraordinary: To me it seems base in the French Historians, to give up the Cause of *Charles* the Ninth, and not to shew the just Reason he had to rid himself of the Admiral and his Accomplices; his Accusation and Sentence were drawn up many Years ago, and afterwards translated into eight Languages; but then came out a second Censure of that Action, which explain'd the former, and shew'd that the Protestants had so often been declared guilty of High Treason, that there was great Cause to applaud these Proceedings, as the only Remedy for the Wars that have happen'd since that time, and perhaps will follow to the end of our Monarchy, if that Maxim of *Cardan* had been pursued, *Nunquam tentabis ut non perficias*, Never attempt, unless you go through with it. You should imitate expert Chirurgeons, who when the Vein is open, let the Blood run even till the Patient faints, to cleanse the Body of all its Humours: It is not sufficient to set out well, but the Course is to be continued, the Reward is at the Goal, and the End regulates the Beginning; however, it may be objected, that there are three Circumstances in this Action, which render it extremely odious to Posterity; the first is, that the Proceeding was not according to the Form of Law; the second, that there was too great an Effusion of Human Blood, and the last, that there were a great many innocent Persons involv'd in the same Fate with the guilty. I shall answer as to the first, that here it is necessary to understand what our Divines say, *De Fide Hæreticis servanda,* how Faith is to be kept with Hereticks; and besides, I shall speak according to my own Opinion, that the *Hugonots* having often broke their Word with us, and having endeavour'd to seize King *Charles* at *Meaux* and other Places, we might render the same to them; and besides, don't we read in *Plato's* fifth Book of his Republick, That they who command, that is to say, Sovereigns, may sometimes cheat and lie, when some extraordinary Benefits may arise from thence to their Subjects. Now could there happen any thing better to *France* than the total Ruin of the Protestants; assuredly, had this Action been omitted, they would have ridicul'd us for the want of Judgment, and we should have been almost as much in Fault, as the Admiral was in coming with the Flower of his Party to be enclos'd in a populous City, that always bore him the utmost hatred, without distrusting the Queen Mother, whose Favourite *Charry* he had slain, or the Family of *Lorrain,* whose Father he had assassinated, nor the King himself, whom he had caused to gallop from *Meaux* to *Paris.* Did not he know that his Religion which was hated even by Persons of the most easie and condescending Temper, could not but be abominated and detested by those Fellows with which he was usually accompany'd; besides, what should hinder, but that the Report that was spread at the same time that they design'd to treat us after the same manner as they were us'd afterwards when their Intrigues were discover'd, might be true; most People think it was true, and for my own part I believe it may be depended upon; as to what concerns the Effusion of Blood, which is said to have been so prodigious, it did not equal that which was shed at *Coutras, St. Denys, Moncontour,* or in several other Slaughters that were made by the *Huguenots*. And whoever shall read in History, that the Inhabitants of *Cæsarea* slew fourscore thousand *Jews* in one Day, that a Million two hundred and forty thousand Persons perish'd in *Judæa* in seven Years time; that *Cæsar* boasts in *Pliny*, that in his foreign Wards he had destroyed a Million a hundred and ninety two thousand Men, and *Pompey* many more in number; that *Quintus Fabius* sent a hundred thousand *Gauls* into the other World, *Caius Marius* two hundred thousand *Cimbers*, *Charles Martel* three hundred thousand *Theutons*, that two thousand Roman Knights, and three hundred Senators, were sacrific'd to the Passion of the *Triumvirat*, four Legions entire to that of *Sylla*, forty thousand Romans to that of *Mithridates*; that *Sempronius Gracchus* ruin'd three hundred Cities in *Spain*, and the *Spaniards* all those in the New World, with more than seven or eight Millions of Inhabitants. I say, whoever will consider all these bloody Tragedies, most of which are to be read in *Justius Lipsius*'s Book of *Constancy*, will find enough to astonish him amidst so many Barbarities, and likewise to make him think that this of St. *Bartholomew* was not one of the greatest, although it was one of the most just and necessary. The third difficulty seems very considerable, seeing a great number of Catholicks were involv'd in the same Tempest, and seem'd to attone for the Death of their Enemies. But the Maxim of *Crassus* in the fourteenth Book of the *Annals of Tacitus*, may serve for an answer in few Words, *Habet aliquid ex iniquo omne magnum exemplum quod contra singulos utilitate publica rependitur*, Every great Example has something in it that is unjust, which as it relates to Particulars, is recompenc'd by the publick Benefit. Whence comes it then that so great an Action, seeing it was both lawful and reasonable, should nevertheless be so much blam'd and cry'd down; as for my self, I attribute the first Cause to have been because it was done by halves, for the *Huguenots* who remain'd could not but disapprove it, and the Catholicks who saw that it seem'd to no purpose, could not forbear saying, that the Enterprize might have been let alone, since they did not go through with it; whereas on the contrary, if all the Hereticks had been massacred, there would none remain at present, at least in *France*, to find fault with it, and the Catholicks likewise would have had no Cause to do it, considering the great Repose and Quiet it would have brought them. The second Reason is, that according to that of the Poet,

> *Segnius irritant animos demissa per aures,*
> *Quam quæ sunt oculis subjecta fidelibus.*

That the Mind is less affected by the Ear, than by that which the Eye is witness of. So we find that they do not speak of this Action in such ill Terms in *Italy*, and other Foreign Parts, as they do in *France*, where it was committed in the midst of *Paris*, and in the Presence of a Million of Persons; and therefore the *Polanders* who receiv'd a particular Narrative of the Fact, from Persons that were the most spiteful and malicious; when the Bishop of *Valence* solicited their Votes for *Henry* the Third, did not make any great difficulty in giving them; because they knew very well that no true Judgment could be made of the natural Temper of a Prince, from one extraordinary and violent Action, to which he had been forc'd by the very just and powerful Reasons of State. I may add, that this Fact is not very far beyond our own Memory, that the greatest part of our Histories have been made since that time by the *Huguenots*, and in short, that we have so large and particular a Description of it in the Memoirs of *Charles* the Ninth; the History of *Beza*, the *Martyrologies*, and several other Books compos'd by Protestants to condemn this Matter, that nothing is forgot to render it blameable and odious; so that it cannot happen otherwise, but that they who hear the Depositions of such corrupt Witnesses should be of their Opinion, although all Persons, who setting aside the little Circumstances can judge without Passion, will be of a contrary Opinion. Besides, no Person can deny but that there were so many factious Persons, and such as bore a Command in their Country, who were put to death upon that Day of St. *Bartholomew*, that from that time the *Huguenots* have not been able to raise Forces from amongst People of their own Persuasion, and that this Blow broke all their Correspondents, all their Cabals and Intriegues that they had both within and without the Kingdom, and indeed, that all their Efforts were inconsiderable, unless sustain'd by the Broils and Seditions of the Catholicks. It is likewise true which some Politicians have remark'd, that the same Day was the cause of a Mischief that could not be expected; for all the Cities, who upon St. *Bartholomew*'s Day perform'd the King's Orders and slew the *Huguenots*, in hopes to procure Peace to the Kingdom, were the first that began the League upon the Account that they were afraid, and not without Reason, that the King of *Navarre*, who was a *Huguenot*, should upon his coming to the Crown, shew some Resentment of the Fact, and for this Cause it may be said, that the Design of St. *Bartholomew* not having been executed so fully as it should, did not only appease the War, for which end it was undertaken, but rais'd another which was still more dangerous.

But to proceed, when there is occasion to give Autority to a Person, and to the Affair that he is concern'd, to raise the Reputation of a Prince, to gain, to bring over or encourage an Undertaker in some important Design; I think for the more easie attaining of such Ends, the Stratagems and refin'd Policies of State may be made use of.

So we see that all the ancient Lawgivers, when they would establish, confirm and authorise the Laws, which they gave their People, thought they could not succeed better than by spreading it abroad with all Industry, and causing it to be believed that they had received them from some Divinity, *Zozoaster* from *Oromasis, Trismegistus* from *Mercury, Zalmoxis* from *Vesta, Charondas* from *Saturn, Minos* from *Jupiter, Lycurgus* from *Apollo, Draco* and *Solon* from *Minerva, Numa* from the Nymph *Egeria, Mahomet* from the Angel *Gabriel;* But *Moses,* who was the most wise of all of them, has describ'd to us in the Book if *Exodus,* how he receiv'd his immediately from God himself. Upon this Consideration, although the Kingdom of the *Jews* be entirely ruin'd and abolish'd, *Mansit tamen* (says *Campanella* in his Political Aphorisms) *Religio Mosaica cum superstitione in* Hebræis & Mahometanis, & cum *reformatione præclarissima in Christianis;* Yet the Mosaical

Religion remained with Superstition amongst the *Hebrews* and *Mahometans*, and with a most excellent Reformation amongst the Christians. And I take this to be the reason why *Cardan* counsels such Princes, as for the Obscurity of their Birth, Want of Money, Partisans or Military Forces, cannot govern their States with sufficient Splendor and Authority, to take the Support of Religion; As was heretofore done with extraordinary Success by *David, Numa* and *Vespasian. Philip* the second of *Spain*, being one of the wisest Princes of his Age, thought of a near Contrivance to give his Son an early Authority amongst those People that he should one day govern: For he made an Edict, that was extremely prejudicial to his Subjects, and let the Rumour be spread from time to time that he would publish and enforce it, upon which the People began to murmur and complain; The King nevertheless persisted in his Resolution, which was likewise followed by the redoubled Complaints of the People; at last the Report comes to the Ears of the *Infant*, who promises to assist the People, and by all means possible to hinder that this Edict should not be published, and to that Effect, he threatened all such as should endeavour to put it in Execution, and omitted nothing that might shew the Desire he had of delivering the People from that Oppression: So that *Philip* having plaid his Game, and speaking no more of the Edict, every one imagined that the Opposition made to it, by the young Prince, was the only Cause of its being supprest; and by this means his Father gain'd him an Empire in the Hearts and Affections of the *Spaniards*, which was more assur'd than that he had over the Kingdoms of both the Spains; *Longe enim valentior est amor ad obtinendum quod velis quam timor,* says *Pliny Junior* in his eighth Epistle. For love is more prevalent in obtaining what you desire than Fear.

In short, if we consider the means that were us'd to convert *Henry* the fourth to the Catholick Religion, and to conform him in it, we shall find a great deal of Conduct, Wit, and Industry throughout the whole Action. For though we ought to hold it for a certain Truth, as may appear by many Testimonies which he gave in his Life time, that it was real, yet if we give our selves the Liberty to consider it as Politicians we may easily remark three things, to wit, the Motives of his Conversion, which were no other than the obstinate Resistance of *Monsieur du Main*, who upon this Occasion in the *Memoirs* of *Tavanes* is said *to have been next under God the sole Author of the Conversion of* Henry *the fourth*; for it is certain that had it not been for him, he might have made a very advantagious Treaty without the change of his Religion. One may likewise place amongst the Motives of this Conversion the Counsel given to the King by Monsieur *de Sully,* one of the principal and most sensible Hugonots in his Army: *That the Crown of* France *was well worth the Trouble of hearing one Mass.* As for what concerns the Circumstances of his Conversion, there were two very remarkable; the first was that the King had not a bigotted or superstitious Divine to instruct and catechise him, who might have made the Entrance of our Churches like to those Porticoes and Vestibles of which the Poet says,

Centauri in foribus stabulant Scyllæque biformes,

There Monsters stand, Centours of double Form.

But by *Rene Prenoust* Doctor of Divinity and Curate of the Parish of St. *Eustace*, who, if one may judge by the common Report, and what happen'd at the point of his Death, was neither an over zealous Catholick, nor an obstinate Heretick; from whence it came to pass, that by a dextrous Management of the King's Conscience, after the same manner as he had done that of his Parishioners for the space of twenty five or thirty Years, he made him only comprehend the principal Mysteries without too large an Heap of the lesser Ceremonies and Traditions; and so manag'd this Conversion, rather like a Man of Prudence and a Politician, than an over scrupulous and superstitious Divine. The second thing remarkable was the Story of *Martha Brossier* a Demoniack, which indeed was only a feign'd Contrivance set on foot by some zealous Catholicks supported by a Cardinal, that the Devil, by which she was said to be possess'd, coming to be driven out by Virtue of the Holy Sacrament, the King shuld take occasion to believe the real Presence in the Eucharist, of which real Presence or rather Transubstantiation, they did not think he was entirely persuaded. But the King who would not let himself be easily surpriz'd before he suffered them to come to Exorcisms, ordered Physitians and Surgeons to be call'd in to give their Advice and Opinion; which being conceiv'd in these Terms, as reported by Monsieur *Marescot* in a little Book that he has publish'd of this Story: *Naturalia multa, ficta Plurima, a Dæmone nulla*, That many of those things proceed from Nature, most from Contrivance, none from the Devil: The poor possessed Creature after having discovered this Ignorance and Brutishness of all the Bigots of *Paris*, was threatned to be whipt out of the Town if she did not depart speedily: Upon which a certain Abbot carried her to *Rome*, from whence Cardinal *d'Ossat* made her retire so suddenly, that she had not time to impose upon any one. The last thing remarkable in this Conversion is what followed afterwards, upon which a Politician who ought to profit and gather Instruction from the least Syllables and Hints given by Historians, may make Reflection upon the Answer of a Peasant to King *Henry*, that *the Pouch will always smell of the Herring*; when being incognito, he ask'd him what the People thought of the King's Conversion; as likewise that of the Mareschal *de Biron*, who being disgusted at the Refusal made him of the Government of *Bourg* in *Bresse,* said to one of his Friends, that if he had been a *Hugonot* it would not have been deny'd him: It is from *Cayer (Book 7. Hist.)* that I have these Remarks, which no one, except a Politician, would look upon as probable, since they are confuted by abundance of others that are directly opposite to them.

Lastly, The Law of Contraries, which ought to be treated of under the same general Head, obliges us to put into this rank the Occasions that may be presented of bounding or ruining the too great Power of a Person, that would abuse it to the Prejudice of the State, or by the great number of his Partisans, and the Cabals of his Correspondents has render'd himself formidable to his Sovereign, so as to dispatch him secretly, without passing through all the Formalities of a regular Justice. It may be done, say the refin'd Politicians, provided that he is guilty and has deserv'd a publick Death, if it was possible to punish him after that manner. The reason upon which *charron* turns this Maxim is, that in this there is nothing violated but the Form, and that the Prince being Master of these Formalities, he may dispense with them as he thinks it necessary. When any one amongst the *Romans*, would by force obtain an Office without the consent of the People, or gave the least suspicion of Aspiring to the Sovereignty, they punish'd him with Death, *Lege Valeria*, by the *Valerian Law*, that is to say, as soon as ever they could and without Form of Justice, which they thought not of till the Execution was over: The famous Lawyer *Ulpian* goes farther, when he says, that *Si forte Latro manifestus, vel seditio prærupta, factioque cruenta vel alia justa causa, moram non recipiunt non pœna festinatione, sed præveniendi periculi causa punire permittit, deinde scribere.* If a manifest Thief, or a Sedition broke forth, or a bloody Faction, or any other just Cause, do not admit of delay, it is permitted to punish, nor to hasten the Punishment, but to prevent the danger, and afterwards to write, that is, to frame the Indictment, or the Formalities of the Accusation. Such were the Executions of *Parmenio* and *Philotas* by *Alexander*, of *Plautian* and *Sejanus* amongst the *Romans*, of *William Mason* in *Sicily*, of the *Messieurs de Guise* and the *Marshall d'Ancre*, under two of our Kings, and of the Collonel of the *Lansquenets* in *Pavia*, who was poisoned by *Antonio de Leva*, because he fomented Trouble and Sedition. Now although these Actions cannot be lawful, but by an extraordinary and absolute Necessity, and that it is Barbarity and Injustice to practise them often, yet the *Spaniards* have nevertheless found means to reconcile them to their Consciences, and to surmount many Difficulties in their Performance. For they appoint secret and private Judges for him that they look upon as a Criminal of State, they make out his Process, they condemn him, and afterwards seek all Methods possible to execute it. *Anthony Rincon* a *Spaniard*, and consequently a Subject of *Charles* the fifth, not being safe in his own Country, came to *Francis* the first, and was sent by him to treat of an Alliance with *Soliman:* The Emperor who foresaw the Damage that might come to him by this Embassy, caus'd *Rincon* and *Cæsar Fregosa,* his Collegue, to be kill'd as they passed down the *Po* to go to *Venice,* by the Contrivance of *Alfonso d'Avalos,* his Lieutenant in the *Milanese:* For which Action the Emperor was so far from thinking him culpable, that even one of our Bishops has pleaded for his Innocence, *Rinco Exul Hispanus & Francisci apud Solimannum legatione functus, non injuria fortasse Fregosus præter jus cæsus videbatur* (Belcar *l.* 22.) *Rincon* a *Spanish* Exile and Envoy from *Francis* to *Soliman,* seems not to have been unjustly slain, tho' the Death of *Fregosa* might be beyond the bounds of Justice.

Andrew Doria having quitted the Party of the King of *France* and taken to that of the Emperor, under whose Favour he held the City of *Genoa,* as a Vassal, *Lewis Fieschi,* a Citizen there undertakes, with the Assistance of *Henry* the Second, and *Peter Louis Farnese,* Duke of *Parma* and *Placentia,* to set the City at Liberty: he kills *Jannetin Doria* immediately, and is drowned by accident when the Enterprise was but just began: what does the Emperor *Charles* the Fifth! upon this incident, he decrees in his Cabinet Councel that *Peter Louis* is guilty of High Treason, and at the same time sends orders to *Doria* to cause him to be assassinated, and to *Gonzaga*, Governor of *Milan*, to seize upon the City of *Placentia*, which was punctually executed according to the Project that was given him, and although the Emperor did all he could possibly to demonstrate, that he had no hand in this Execution, yet all Historians write the contrary, and the Distick mentioned by *Noel des Comptes*, shews sufficiently that it was believed to be so in those times,

> *Cæsaris* injussu *cecidit* Farnesius *Heros*,
> 　　*Sed Data sund jussu præmia sicariis.*

> *Cæsar* gave no command *Farnese* shou'd bleed,
> But paid the Villains who perform'd the Deed.

But to proceed: Was not the Cardinal *George* of *Hungary* sentenc'd after the same manner, and executed with more barbarity by *Ferdinand* of *Austria*, upon a suspicious Fear which he had conceiv'd, that the Cardinal would seek Assistance from the *Turk* to continue his Command in *Transylvania?* And have we not seen within these four Years; that *Walestein* was assassinated in *Egra* by the secret Management of the Count *D'Ognate*, who was then Embassador from the King of *Spain* to the Emperor? And that the Burgomaster *La Ruelle* was treated after the same sort in the Town of *Liege* by the Count *De Warfuzée*, pursuant to the Orders that had been given him by the Marquis *D'Aytone*, Commander of the Armies in the *Low-Countries*, with such precise Formalities that even those of making him die, *after Confession and Resignation to the Will of God,* were not omitted, to add the greater Strength to the Action, and to make it appear like a Criminal Sentence that had been lawfully given and executed. In short, this kind of Justice is so much in Fashion in the Houses of *Austria* and *Spain,* that even the Father would not exempt his own Son from it, when he judg'd it less expedient for the good of his Kingdom to let him live than die. *Cætera enim Maleficia tunc persequare cum facta sunt, hoc nisi provideris ne accidat ubi evenit, frustra judicia explores,* as *Cato* said very well in his Oration concerning *Cataline*'s Conspiracy in *Salust,* You may prosecute other Crimes when they are perpetrated, but unless you prevent this before it happens, when it is once committed it will be in vain to seek for Judgment against the Actors of it. And it were to be wish'd that the great Emperor *Charles* the *Fifth,* who perform'd so many master Strokes of State, had not been short in that which he should have put in practice upon *Luther*'s Person, when he appear'd at the Conference of *Ausbourg!* we should not now be forc'd to cry out with *Lucan,*

> *Heu quantum Terræ potuit Pelagiq; parari,*
> *Hoc quem civiles fuderunt sanguine dextra.*

What Countries might not have been subdued by the Expence of the Blood and Treasure which the Civil Wars have consum'd.

But not to speak of *Germany* and other foreign Countries, *Bodin* and divers Authors have shown, that since the first Tumults rais'd by the *Calvinists* till the Reign of *Henry* the *Fourth,* the pretended Reform'd, have given us five most cruel and bloody Battels, and have been the cause of the Death of above a Million of People; of the surprizal of three hundred Towns; of the Expence of a hundred and fifty Millions only for the payment of the Troops; and that nine Cities, four hundred Villages, twenty thousand Churches, two thousand Monasteries, and ten thousand Houses have been entirely burnt or ruin'd. To which if one should add all that has happen'd in the last Wars with the present King, I am assur'd one might erect a spectacle of Horror capable of moving Compassion in the hardest Hearts, and drawing this Exclamation from Persons of the most reserv'd Expressions:

Tantum Religio potuit suadere malorum,

Religion to such Mischiefs can persuade.

Now seeing no Person as yet has made Reflection upon this History of *Luther*, I shall say in my Opinion, that they made three very false Steps when he began to publish his Heresies; the first was, in suffering him to pass from the Correction of Manners to that of Doctrine; seeing in that case, what is most common is always the best, and that to change any thing in it is dangerous and of little Profit, that it is not for a private Person to do it. And in short, that a Christian Kingdom well order'd ought never to receive any other Novelties in Religion, than such as the Popes and Councils have been accustom'd to introduce, from time to time, to accommodate them to the Necessities of the Church; which Church ought to be the only Rule of holy Scripture and our Faith, as the Councils are of the Church, and amongst the Councils that which was celebrated last ought to be prefer'd to all those which preceded it. The second was, that *Luther* being come to *Ausbourg* with a real design to confer, and if possible, to agree with the Catholicks, the Cardinal *Cajetan* ought to have accepted the Offers that he made, not to say or write any more in the matter they were treating of, provided reciprocally that they should impose Silence upon *Ecchius, Cochleus, Sylvester, Prierias,* and others of his Adversaries: And not to have press'd him to deny or recant in Publick all that he had said or preach'd to the People with so much Ardor and Vehemence. After which the third was, that they had not recourse to some Master-Piece of State, when they saw he began to champ upon the Bitt and grow resty at the indiscreet Zeal of the Legat. For they should have stopt his Mouth, his Tongue should have been softned with *Spread Eagles,* since *Oxen* and *Syrenes,* that have *been often prevalent on such occasions, are no longer now in Fashion,* that is to say, they ought to have gain'd him by some good Benefice or Pension, as they did afterwards by several learned and celebrated Ministers. *Ferrier* about thirty Years ago undertook an odd Enterprize of going to *Rome,* to maintain the Doctrine, that the Pope was Anti-christ; and yet the Queen-Mother had no great Trouble in making him quit his Party and come over to us. And Monsieur the Cardinal *de Richelieu* had never accomplish'd so many glorious Undertakings against the *Huguenots,* if he had not made use of the King's Revenues to gain their greatest Generals. So true is that saying of *Horace,*

Aurum per medios ire satellites

Et perrumpere amat saxa
Ictu fulmineo.   (Ode 16 l. 3.)

Gold through Guards can go,
Walls with ease can overthrow
By the fierce Thunder of its Blow.

But if *Luther* could not have been managed by this means, they should have made use of another and secur'd his Person, as they did lately to the Abbot *du Bois,* and *Barnese* the *Benedictine,* or else have gone farther, and dispatch'd him secretly, as it is said *Katherine de Medicis* did a famous Magician; either publickly and by Form of Justice, as the Fathers of the Council of *Constance* did *John Hus* and *Jerom* of *Prague:* though to say true, the first Means were the most proper, since they were more moderate, easy, and private; and such as might more certainly produce the Effect that was aim'd at, which the last could not do, but might perhaps have exasperated the Duke of *Saxony,* and confirm'd the Followers of *Luther* in their false Opinions; for what was said of the ancient Christians, *Sanguis Martyrum est semen Christianorum,* The Blood of the Martyrs is the Seed of Christians; may be applied to all those who have once begun to maintain those Opinions which they persuade themselves to be true. And in effect *Henry* the *Second* thinking by this sort of Punishment not only to stifle Heresy, but to prevent the occasions that foreign Princes might one Day take, of disturbing his Kingdom by the Means of the *Calvinists,* as he had perplex'd and embroil'd them, by assisting the *Lutherans* in *Germany,* was very much deceiv'd; for the number of Hereticks increas'd daily, so that they put the whole Kingdom in Confusion under *Charles* the *Ninth:* and *Henry* the *Third* being necessitated to make use of their Forces, so rais'd the Choler and indiscreet zeal of *Jacobin*, that he despis'd the losing of his own Life, so he might take away that of his Prince. The learned Mathematician *Regiomontanus*, being sent for from *Germany* to *Rome*, to reform the Calendar, died there in the very height of his Labour; and if his Friends and the Hereticks may be believ'd, it was a piece of Policy of *gregory* the *Thirteenth,* who had rather make use of his Goblet than see his Design, and the Work of the most expert Astronomers in *Italy* not only retarded, but entirely overthrown by the opposition of so learned a Person. But it is certain that the Death of *Regiomontanus* ought in no wise to blemish the Innocence of so good and generous a Pope, since it was rather a Crime committed by the Sons of *George Trapezuntius*, who being griev'd for their Father's Death, and thinking that *Regiomontanus* was the Cause of it, by having made too severe Remarks upon the Latin Translation of *Ptolomey*'s *Almagest*, set forth by *Trapezuntius*, they resolv'd to be reveng'd of him and treated him rather after a *Greek* manner than a *Roman*. If the *Venetians* had been as innocent of the Death of *Lauredan,* one of their Citizens, *Bodin* (Book 6.) would not have remark'd in his *Method*, that he did not live long after he had appeas'd, by his Presence only a furious Sedition of the Mariners embru'd with te Blood of the Mechanicks, when all the Magistrates and the whole Forces of the City assembled, could not remedy the Confusion. Perhaps they were afraid, that coming to understand his own Power, and the Command he had over the Subjects of the Republick, he should have the Ambition of making himself absolute Master of their State: Perhaps likewise they did it out of Jealousy and Emulation, as *Aristotle* says the *Argonauts* would not let *Hercules* go in their Company, for fear all the Glory of so great an Enterprize should be attributed only to his Valour and Virtue,

> *Urit enim fulgore suo qui prægravat Artes*
> *Infra se positas.*   (Hor. Ep. Book 2. Ep. I.)

A superior Excellency in any Art will always create Envy, and its Brightness will be too strong to be endur'd b those below it.

And the same *Aristotle* adds, that the *Ephesians* banish'd *Hermodorus*, their Prince, because he was too good a Man. This was the Reason which establish'd the *Ostracism* at *Athens*, and oblig'd *Scipio* and *Hannibal* to put to Death two brave Soldiers, who were their Prisoners. Now if the Stratagem be true, which it is said that the *Venetians* made use of not long ago, when they spread the Report that the Duke *d'Ossuna* had some Enterprize in hand against their City, I look upon it as one of the most Judicious that I have mention'd: Besides it was of great Importance to them to do it, to oblige the Embassador of one of the greatest Princes in *Europe*, to quit his Practices, that aim'd at nothing less than the Ruine of their State, and force him afterwards to a decent Retreat. So it is that those sovereign Remedies ought to be reserv'd for dangerous Maladies, and to be made use of, as *Horace* says the *Gods should be, who are introduc'd into Tragedies, to perfect and finish that which Mortals could not effect,*

Nec Deus intersit nisi dignus Vindice nodus Adfuerit.
(Horace Art of Poetry.)

Or as Mariners do by their Sheet Anchor, which they never throw into the Sea till all other hopes is given over. For in truth, if a Counsellor or Minister should propose to himself to get out of all the Difficulties that present themselves to him by some one of these Expedients, he would be look'd upon as no less wicked and foolish than a Surgeon that would Cure every Hurt by burning or cutting off the Member that had receiv'd it. *Extremis siquidem malis extrema Remedia adhibenda sunt*, Extraordinary Remedies are to be applied to extraordinary Diseases. I farther add, that if the same Counsellor abuses these Remedies to support his own Interests, or to give a freer Range to his Passions, besides the betraying of his Master's Service, he becomes guilty before God and Man of the Evil he attempts to do. And the Sovereign himself when he uses these sorts of Politicks, otherwise than for the good of the Publick or his own, which is not to be separated from what the other requires, he rather acts according to the Passion and Ambition of a Tyrant, than performs the Office of a King. So we see that Queen *Katherine* of *Medicis, Quam exitio patriæ natam Mathematici dixerun*, Who by the Astrologers was said to be born for the Destruction of her Country; could not bear being married to the Son of a King without being a Queen, and therefore made use of the Artifice of one *Montecuculi*, to get rid of the only Obstacle she had in the

114

Person of her Husband's elder Brother, *Affinitatem enim nuper cum Clemente contractam tanto sceleri causam dedisse postea compertum, quamvis inscio marito; verum illo Mortuo cum frater proximus esset, qui in Regnum succederet, omissa indagandæ rei cura est & suppressa veritas;* For it was afterwards found out that the Affinity lately contracted with *Clement* was the Cause of all that Villany, but transacted without her Husband's Knowledge; but when he was dead, and the Brother was the next to succeed him in the Kingdom, there was little Care taken of searching into the Matter, but the Truth was suppress'd and stifled, as *Thuanus*has very well remark'd in his original History. She afterwards undertook the Protection of the Hereticks by Letters and secret Advices, to Balance the Power of the *Constable* and Monsieur *de Guise*, in who Assassination, which happen'd before *Orleance*, the *Memoires* of *Tavanes* say, that she boasted to have had a part, as she had likewise afterwards in that of the Admiral; not but that she had other Motives for all these bloody Tragedies, besides the desire of satisfying her Ambition; the Reigning under the Name of her Children, and the keeping up an Enmity between those Persons whose Authority might in any measure over-shadow her own.

CHAP. IV. *What Opinions are necessary to be held by them who make use of these Refin'd Politicks.*

IT is not enough to have shewn the Occasions there may be for undertaking these Stratagems, if we do not go farther and show what Notions and Persuasions People ought to have to execute them with Boldness, and to bring them to a happy Conclusion. And although this Title seems rather to belong to the Qualities and Conditions of the Minister who may advise them, I shall not however desist from laying down in this place such as are the principal ones, since they are Maxims most certain, universal, and infallible; which not only Counsellors, but Princes and all sorts of Persons of good Sense and Judgment ought to follow and observe in all Affairs that may happen to them; and for want of which the Reasonings made in Matters of State are often Lame and Misshapen, and are rather like the Tales of old Women, and gross Mechanicks, than the Discourses of wise Persons, and such as have had Experience in the Affairs of the World.

Boethius, that great Councellor of State to King *Theodoric,* furnishes us with the first of them, which he delivers in these Terms in his Book of Consolation, *Constat, æterna positumq; lege est, in mundo constans genitum esse nihil,* It is a Maxim establish'd upon an eternal Law, that nothing born into the World is constant. To which likewise agrees that saying of St. *Jerom* in his Epistle. *Omnia orta occidunt, & Aucta senescunt,* All things die that are born, and grow old that receive an increase. The Poets were of the same Opinion,

> *Immortale nihil mundi compagetenetur.*
> *Non Urbes non Regna hominum, non Aurea Roma.*

> Nothing within this Universal Frame,
> Is form'd by Nature to be still the same,
> Not Towns or Empires can their Lustre hold,
> And *Rome* must fade, though now adorn'd with

Gold.

Nor can any Persons differ from it, who seriously consider how this great Circle of the Universe, since it has first began its Course, has not ceas'd to introduce and change Monarchies, Religions, Sects, Cities, Men, Beasts, Trees, Stones, and generally all that is comprehended in this vast Machine; nor are the Heavens themselves free from their Change and their Corruption; the first Empire of the *Assyrians*, that of the *Persians* which followed, were likewise the first that ceas'd, the *Greek* and *Roman* were not of much longer Duration. The potent Families of *Ptolomy, Attalus* and *Seleucus*, are nothing now but Stories.

> *Miramur periisse homoines? Monumenta fatiscunt,*
> *Mors etiam saxis Nominibusque venit.*

> Wonder we then at Mens Mortality,

When Monuments, and Stones, and Names must die.

The Isle of *Crete*, were there were an hundred Cities, the City of *Thebes* which had an hundred Gates, that *Troy* which was built by the Hands of the Gods, that *Rome* which triumph'd over the World, where are they now? *Jam Segest est ubi Troja fuit*, Corn grows upon their Ruins. We ought not therefore to run into the Error of those weak Spirits, who imagine that *Rome* will always be the Seat of the Holy Fathers, and *Paris* that of the Kings of *France*; *Byzantium illud vides quod sibi placet duplici imperii sede? Venetias istas quæ superbiunt mille annorum firmitate? Veniet illis sua dies, & Tu Antwerpia, Ocelle urbium, aliquando non eris!* Do you see *Byzantium*, that is, *Constantinople*, proud of having been the Seat of so many Empires? Or *Venice*, that glories in a thousand Years continuance; their Periods shall come, and there will be a time when it shall be said of thee, *Antwerp*, the Delight of our Eyes, the brightest of Cities, that *Antwerp* was! as that judicious Author *Justus Lipsius* has express'd it, Since then this Maxim is so true, a great Spirit will never despair of being able to surmount all the Difficulties which would perhaps deter another, from executing or undertaking any Affairs of great importance; as for Example, if the Question should be, that a Minister either for the Service of God or his Master, should think of Measures to ruin some Republick or Empire, this general Maxim will make him believe immediately that such an Enterprize is not impossible, since there is none of them that has the Privilege of enduring and subsisting always; and on the contrary, if the Matter be to establish a State, he may make use of the same Maxim to confirm his Resolution of undertaking it, and persuade himself that he may as easily attain his end as the *Switzers*, the *Lucchese*, the *Hollanders*, and the People of *Geneva* have done, not in Ages beyond our Memory, but in these latter ones, and within the Compass of our own Knowledge; so it is with the States, as it is with Men, one dies, another is born, one is stifled in the beginning, others grow up and gather Force and a good Constitution, at the Expence of their Neighbours, many pass even to old Age, but at last their Strength fails them, they give place to others, and quit their Post because they can no longer defend it.

> *Sic omnia verti*
> *Cernimus atque alias assumere pondera gentes.*
> *Concidere has.*

> So we see all things turn, and in the Scale,
> Some Nations sink, whilst other States prevail.

And then the first Distempers move them, the second shock them, and the third carry them off; *Gracchus, Sertorius, Spartacus*, gave the first Blow to the Roman Commonwealth, *Sylla, Marius*, and *Julius Cæsar* made it totter, so as to be within two Fingers breadth of its Ruin, and *Augustus*, after the Furies of the Triumvirate buried it, *Urgentibus scilicet Romani imperii fatis*, for so the Fates required; and from the most famous Republick of the World, made it the greatest Empire; just as from the greatest Empires that are at present, there will one day arise the most powerful Republicks. But it must likewise be observed, that these Changes, these Revolutions of States, this Death of Empires, cannot be effected, without drawing along with it the Laws, the Religion, and the Sects; if it were not more reasonable to say, that these three internal Principles of State happening to grow old and be corrupted, the Religion by Heresie or Atheism, Justice by the Sale of Offices, the Countenance of great Persons, or the Authority of Sovereigns; and the Sects by the Liberty which every one takes of introducing new Opinions, or reviving old Ones, they likewise cause all that to fall and perish which was built upon them, and dispose of Affairs so as they may admit of some Change or considerable Revolution. And indeed, if we consider the Sate which *Europe* is in at present, it will not be difficult to foresee that it is likely in a short time to be the Theatre on which many such Tragedies will be acted, since the greatest part of the States which it contains, are very near that Age which has been fatal to others; and that such long and destructive Wars have rais'd and increas'd the Causes before-mention'd, which may ruin Justice; as the great number of Colleges, Seminaries, Scholars, with the liberty of printing and importing Books, have already shaken Religion, and the several Sects of it. And it is a thing beyond dispute, that the Systems of Astronomy are more encreas'd, more Novelties in Philosophy, Medicine and Theology have been propagated, that the number of Atheists has appear'd much greater since the ear 1452, when after the taking of *Constantinople*, the Greeks and the Sciences together with them found Refuge in *Europe*, and particularly in *France* and *Italy*, than had been during the thousand Years preceding. As for my self, I defie the most knowing in the

French History, to shew that any one was accus'd of Atheism, before the Reign of *Francis* the First, sirnam'd the Restorer of Letters, and perhaps it would be difficult to find me one in *Italy*, before *Cosimus* and *Laurence de Medicis* gave Encouragement to Men of Learning. It was in the Age of *Augustus*, that *Horace* said of himself, (*Ode* 34. *Book* I.)

> *Parcus deorum cultor & infrequens*
> > *Insanientis dum sapientiæ*
> *Consultus erro.*

> With small Devotion, scanty Prayer,
> > I to the Gods address;
> Wild Schemes of Wisdom I prepare,
> > And erring do profess.

That *Lucretius* thought to gain the good Will of his Reader, by telling them he would deliver them from the Bonds, Racks and Torments which Religion gave them.

> *Dum Religionum animos vinclis exsolvere pergo.*

> Whilst from Religions Bonds I loose your minds,

And that St. *Paul* said to the *Romans, Tunc veni cum Deus non erat in vobis*, that he came to them when they were as yet without God. In short, it was under the Kings *Almansor* and *Miramolin*, the most studious and learned of their Predecessors, that the *Aladinistes* or Libertines were in so great Vogue amongst the *Arabians*; so that we may say with *Seneca, Ut rerum omnium sic literatrum intemperantia laboramus*, as in all other things, so we labour with an Excess and Intemperance in Learning.

The second Opinion that we ought to be persuaded of to obtain Success in these Master Strokes of Policy, is to believe that there is no necessity of overturning the whole World, to occasion the Changes of the greatest Empires, they very often happen without ones thinking of them, or at least without making great Preparations for them. And as *Archimedes* could move the greatest Weights, by three or four pieces of Timber join'd together according to Art, so one may ruine, or bring about the greatest Affairs, by means that seem to be almost of no Consideration. *Cicero* in his fifth *Philippick*, gives us a hint of this, when he says, *Quis nesciat minimis fieri momentis maximas temporis inclinationes*; Who does not know that the greatest Variations of Time proceed from the minutest Moments. The World, according to the Doctrine of *Moses* was made of nothing, and according to that of *Epicurus*, it was compos'd of the Concourse of diverse Atoms; and those great Rivers which flow with such Impetuousness, almost from one end of the Continent to the other, are ordinarily so small at their beginning, that it is not easie to trace them.

Flumina quanta vides parvis e fontibus orta.

See what vast Streams rise from small trickling Springs.

It happens often in Politicks, that a little Spark neglected, oftentimes rises to a great Fire.

Dum neglecta solent incendia sumere vires.

'Tis by Neglect that Fires assume their Strength.

And as a small Stone cut out of the Mountain, was sufficient to break the Statue, or rather the Colossus of *Nebuchadnezzar*, so a little thing may easily overthrow the greatest Monarchies: Who would ever have believed that the Rape of *Helen*, the ravishing of *Lucretia* by *Tarquin*, and that of the Daughter of Count *Julian* by King *Roderick*, should have produc'd such notable Effects in *Greece, Italy* and *Spain*; but who would ever have thought that the *Ætolians* and *Arcadians* should have enter'd into so bloody a War for the Head of a Boar; that the People of *Carthage* and *Brisagne* should do the same for the Hulk of a Brigantine; the Duke of *Burgundy* and the *Switzers* for a Load of Sheeps Skins; the *Frisons* and the *Romans* in the time of *Drusus* for some Ox Hides; and the *Picts* and *Scots* for some Dogs that were missing? Or that in the time of the Emperor *Justinian*, all the Cities in the Empire should be divided, and conceive a mortal Hatred against one another, for the difference of the Colours that were us'd in their publick Shews and Recreations? This sort of proceeding seems to be agreeable to Nature, when it produces the lofty and spatious Cedars from a little Bud, and Elephants and Whales from that Seed, which in comparison to them is but an Atom. In this it endeavours to imitate its Creator, who uses to draw the Grandeur of his Actions from the Weakness of their Beginnings, and to carry them on from a feeble Original to an accomplish'd Perfection: Therefore when he would deliver his People from the Captivity of *Pharaoh*, he did not send some King or Prince attended with a numerous Army, but he made use of a plain Man, *Impeditioris & Tardioris Linguæ qui pascebat oves* Jethro *soceri sui*, Slow of Speech and of a slow Tongue, who fed the Sheep of *Jethro* his Father-in-law, *Exod.* iii. 4. When he would chastise and terrify the *Ægyptians*, he did not make use of Lightning and Thunder, *Sed immisit tanum Ranas, & Cyniphes & Locustas, & omne genus muscarum*, But sent Frogs, Lice, Locusts, and swarms of Flies amongst them. When he would deliver his People from the *Philistine*, it was by the Hands of *Saul*, whom he commanded to be crown'd King of his People, at the same time that he thought of nothing but *looking after the Asses of Kish his Father,* 1 Sam. x. So to fight *Goliath* he chose *David* whilst he kept his Father's Flocks, *Ch.* xvii. And to deliver *Bethulia* from the Army of *Holofernes*, he did not employ well appointed and valiant Soldiers, but he *broke down their stateliness by the Hands of a Woman,* Judith ix. But since these Actions are so many Miracles, and therefore we can draw no Consequence from them, let us make some Reflection upon the Empire of the *Turks*, and the marvellous Progresses that are that are made every Day by the *Lutehrans and Calvinists,* and I am certain we shall be forc'd to admire how the Spightfulness of two Monks, who had no other Weapons but their Pens and their Tongues, should have been the Cause of so great Revolutions and such extraordinary Changes in Policy and Religion. After which it must be confess'd that the Embassadors of the *Scythians* had good reason to remonstrate to *Alexander*, that *Fortis Leo aliquando minimarum avium pabulum est, ferrum rubigo consumit, & nihil est cui periculum non immineat ab invalido*, The magnanimous Lion is the Food of the smallest Birds: Rust consumes Iron, and there is nothing but what is endanger'd by that which is much weaker than itself. It is therefore the Duty of a right Politician, to consider all the small Circumstances which are to be met with in Affairs that are serious and difficult, to make use of an enlarge them by making a Flie sometimes become an Elephant, by turning a Scratch into a Wound, and a Spark into a Fire; or else by diminishing all things as it shall be proper to favour his Intentions. And to this purpose I remember an Accident which has not been much taken notice of, that pass'd in the Assembly of the Estates held at *Paris* in the Year 1615, which nevertheless might have ruin'd *France* and chang'd the Form of its Government, if it had not been quickly remedied; for the Nobility having inserted into their Bundle of Remonstrances, an Article to set forth the Benefit that would accrue to *France* by abolishing annual Right, or the *Pollet.* The third State, which look'd upon themselves to be greatly griev'd by this Proposal, put in another Clause in their Remonstrance, by which they pray'd the King to retrench the Pensions that he gave to a great many Gentlemen who did him no Service. Upon this each Party began to maintain their Point, and both sent Deputies to set for their Reasons; they met, and then came to high Words and ill Language; the Deputies of the Nobility calling those of the third Estate Rusticks, and threatning to kill them. The others answer'd that they durst not do it, and if they should be think of it, they had a hundred thousand Men in *Paris* who would bring them to Reason immediately. In the mean time some Magistrates and Ecclesiasticks who were present at this Discourse, foreseeing the dangerous Consequences that might follow, ride with full speed to the *Louvre* and advise the King of what had happen'd, pray and entreat him to apply some speedy Remedy; and prevail so far, that the King, the Queens, and all the Princes interpose their Authority; and it is prohibited under Pain of Death, to speak of these two Articles, or to discourse of any thing that had happen'd in relation to them; and happy it was that Matters were so easily compos'd: For as the Deputies of the Nobility had pass'd from Words to Actions, they of the third State might have prov'd so violent, obstinate, revengeful, and the People of *Paris* being in such a Disposition and Ferment, that all the Nobility who were there had run a great Risque of being cut to pieces; and perhaps the like might have been done throughout all the other Cities in the Kingdom, which generally follow the Example of the Capital.

Now seeing this Accident, if not prevented, would have been perform'd by the Means of the Populace, who nor judging or knowing what Reason is would have thrown themselves without Fear or Understanding, upon the first that had stood in the way of their Fury. It is not foreign to the purpose to take notice of, and place it as a third Persuasion, that the greatest Master-Strokes of States being done by them, one ought to know particularly what their Nature is, and with what Boldness and Assurance they may be made use of, and turn'd and dispos'd for any Design. They who have made the fullest and most exact Description of them, represent them justly as a Monster with many Heads, inconstant, wandring, foolish, stupid, without Conduct, Wit, or Judgment. As for its Reason *Palingenius* says,

> *Judicium vulgi insulsum imbecillaq; mens est.*

Foolish their Judgment and their Reason weak.

As for its Passions, the same Author adds

> *Quod furit atque ferit savissima Bellua vulgus.*

The cruel Beast the Mob with Fury strikes.

If we look upon his Manners and way of acting, *Hi Vulgi mores odisse præsentia, ventura cupere, præterita celebrare*, to hate things present, desire those to come, and to extol whatever is past. *Salust* represents it to us *Ingenio Mobile, seditiosam, discordiosam, cupidam rerum novarum, quiete & otio adversami*, Of a variable Temper, seditious, contentious, desirous of Novelty, and an Enemy to Rest and Quietness. But I shall go farther and say, that it is inferior to Beasts and worse than Beasts, and an hundred times more stupid; for Beasts not having the use of Reason, leave themselves to be guided by the Instinct which Nature gives them for the Rule of their Life, Passions, and Modes of Acting, from which they never depart unless the Wickedness of Man causes them to do it. Whereas the People (I understand by this word Mob, gather'd into a Body, the Dregs of a Nation, Persons of a base, servile and mean Condition) being endowed with Reason, abuse it after a thousand ways, and so become the Theatre where the Orators, Preachers, false Prophets, Impostors, crafty Politicians, Mutineers, the Seditious, the Malicious, the Superstitious, and the Ambitious, and in short, all those who have any new Design, represent their most horrid and bloody Tragedies. We should likewise know that this Populace is compar'd to a Sea agitated with all sorts of Winds and Tempests, to the *Camelion* which can appear in all sorts of Colours, except the White, and to a Sink that all the Refuse of the House is thrown into: Its best Qualities are to be inconstant and variable, to approve and disapprove a thing at the same time, to run always from one contrariety to another, to believe groundlessly, Mutiny readily, Grumble and Murmur incessantly: In short, whatever it thinks is nothing but Vanity, all that is says is False and Absurd, what it dislikes is Good, what it practises is Evil, what it praises is Infamous, and all that it undertakes is pure Folly. This has made *Seneca* say (in his Book of a Happy Life, *ch.* 8.) *Non tam bene cum rebus humanis geritur, ut meliora pluribus placeant, Argumentum pessimi est Turba.* Human Affairs are not so transacted as that the Best should please the most, for the Multitude is an Argument directly to the contrary. And the same Author gives us no other Advice to know what Opinions are good and solid, *Quid solidum crepet,* but only not to follow those of the Vulgar *sanabimur si modo seperemur a cætu.* Let *Postellus* persuade it that *Jesus Christ* was to save the Men, and his Mother *Joan* was to save the Women, it will presently believe him. Let *David George* say he is the Son of God, it will adore him. Let an Enthusiastick Tailor at *Munster* set himself up for a King, and say, that God had predestinated him to chastize all the Powers upon Earth, it shall obey and respect him as the greatest Monarch in the World. Let Father *Domptius* declare that Anti-christ is come, that he is ten Years old and has Horns, it will be frighted at him. Let Impostors and Mountebanks give themselves the Title of *Rosycrucians*, it will run after them. Let the Story go that *Paris* shall be swallowed up, it will fly away; that all the World shall be drown'd it will presently make Arks and Boats not to be surpriz'd; that the Sea shall be dried up, and Chariots may go from *Genoa* to *Jerusalem*, it will prepare for the Journey. Tell it the Fables of *Melusine*, of the *Sabat*, of the *Sorcerers*, of Men turn'd to Wolves, of Fairies, Spectres and Hobgoblins, it will wonder at them. Let the Fits of the Mother torment a poor Girl, it will say she is possest, or will trust to some ignorant or wicked Priest that tells it so. Let some Alchymist, Magician, Astrologer, Lullist or Cabalist begin to shew their Tricks, it will take them for the most knowing and honest Persons in the World. Let *Peter* the *Hermit* come and preach the *Crusade*, it will make Relicks of the Hairs of his Mule. Let a Plague or Tempest ruin a Province it will immediately accuse the Witches or Magicians. In short, if one deceive or baffle it to Day, it will suffer it self to be surpriz'd again to Morrow, never drawing any Advantage from what has pass'd to govern it self either at present or for the future; and in these things consist the principal signs of its great Indiscretion and Weakness. As for its Inconstancy we have a signal Example in the Acts of the Apostles, when the Inhabitants of *Lystra* and *Derbe had seen what* Paul *had done, they lift up their Voices, saying, in the Speech of* Lycaonia, *the Gods are come down to us in the Likeness of*

Men, and they call'd Barnabas Jupiter, *and* Paul Mercury, *Acts* 14. And yet it was but a small time afterwards, *when having ston'd* Paul, *they drew him out of the City supposing he had been dead,* (ibid.) The *Romans* in the Morning ador'd *Sejanus* and before Night *Ducitur unco spectandus,* he is drag'd about the City like a Traytor. The *Parisians* did so by the Marquis *d'Ancre,* and when they had endeavour'd to get pieces of the Robe of the Father *Jesus Maria,* to preserve as Relicks within two Days after they had ridicul'd and made a Jest of him. If it pretends to be angry it is like the young Man in *Horace,*

> *———Iram*
> *Colligit & ponit temere, mutatur in horas.*

Who is rais'd to the height of Passion, and is pacified as easily, being as variable as the Time he changes in. If it meets with a Man of Authority when it is in the highest ferment of its Mutiny and Sedition, it will fly and abandon every thing: But if some headstrong Fellow presents himself, who had put a new Heart in them and blow up the Cinders, they become more furious than they were in the first Rencounter. In short, we may particularly attribute it to that which *Seneca* (in his Book of a happy Life) says of all Mankind, *Fluctuat, aliud ex alio comprehendit, petita relinquit, alternæ inter cupiditatem suam & pœnitentiam vices sunt,* He is always wavering, lays hold of one thing, then of another, relinquishes what he sought, then redemands what he relinquish'd; there being an alternate Vicissitude between his Desires and Repentance. Now forasmuch as strength lies on this side, and that it is this

Creature that can give the greatest turn to all that happens extraordinary in a State, it is necessary that Princes or their Ministers should study how to manage and persuade them by fair Words, to seduce and deceive them by fair Words, to seduce and deceive them by Appearances; to gain them over and bring them into their Interest by Preachers and Miracles, under the pretext of Sanctity, or by the means of able Pens, that may compose clandestine Books, Manifesto's, Apologies, and Declarations, artfully worded to lead them by the Nose and make them approve or condemn whatever is contain'd in the whole Proceedings. But as there were never but two ways possible to keep Men in their Duty, that is, the regard of Punishments establish'd by ancient Legislators, to repress Crimes, of which Judges might take Cognizance; and the Fear of the Gods and their Thunder to restrain those things of which, for want of Witnesses, they cannot be sufficiently inform'd, agreeable to that of the Poet *Palingenius*,

> *Semiferum vulgus frænandum est Religione*
> *Pænarumq; metu, nam fallax atq; malignum*
> *Illius ingenium est semper nec sponte movetur*
> *Ad rectum.*

> The brutish Mob, led by a perverse Will,
> Is fond of Fraud, and every thing that's ill;
> Its secret Faults Religion must restrain,
> Its other Crimes are curb'd by outward Pain.

The same Legislators have acknowledg'd, that there is nothing that has so much Dominion over the Spirits of the

People as this latter; which finding that it self is aim'd at in any Action, pushes it on immediately to the utmost Extremity; Prudence is chang'd into Passion, Choler into Rage, all manner of Conduct runs into Confusion; Goods and Life never come under Consideration whether they are lost or no; to defend the Divinity of an Ape's Tooth, an Ox, a Cat, or an Onyon, or any other Idol, though more ridiculous. *Nulla siquidem res efficacius multitudinem movet quam superstitio;* (Quintus Curtius, *Book IV.*) *Nothing is so powerful in stirring up the Multitude as Superstition.* And in effect this has always been the Mask to the Cheats and Contrivances that have been practis'd in the three different sorts of Life, to which, as has been said before, these Master-strokes of State ma have any relation. For as yet to the Monastick we have an Example in St. *Jerom's* Epistles, (*Book II. ch.* 13.) of the old Monks of *Thebes, They feign Stories of their fighting with Devils, that amongst the Unskilful and Vulgar they may seem to do Miracles, and so to encrease their Gain.* To which we may refer that Deceit which the Priests of the God *Canopus* made use of to render him superior to the *Fire*, that was the God of the *Persians*. That of the *Roman* Knight to enjoy the fair *Paulina* under the Name of *Æsculapius*, the feigned Visions of the *Jacobins* of *Bern*, the false Apparitions of the *Cordeliers* of *Orleans*, which are too common to be recited here at large. If it be doubted if such an Abuse may be in OEconomy, one need only read what Rabbi *Moses* writes of the Priests of the Idol *Thamuz*, or *Adonis*, who to encrease their Offerings, often caus'd him to weep for the Iniquities of the People, but it was with Tears of Lead, melted by a Fire kindled behind the Image: Or what is in *Daniel*, how he strew'd the

Pavement of the Idol *Bel* with Ashes, and so discover'd how the Priests, with their Wives and Children, came in the Night by subterraneous Passages, and eat all that, which the credulous People thought had been devour'd by that Deity. Lastly, that which regards Politicks shall be something more largely express'd, because it is the principal Design, and show how Princes and their Ministers, *Quibus quæstui sunt capti superstitione animi,* (*Livy*, Book IV.) *who make their Advantage of such Persons as are enclin'd to Bigotry,* have known how to manage Religion, and to make use of it as the most easy and certain means by which they might accomplish their greatest Enterprizes: They seem to have made use of it in five especial manners, under which several lesser matters may be rang'd. The first and most common is that of all Legislators and Politicians, who have persuaded their People, that they had Communication with the Gods, that so they might put their Designs in Execution; as we see that, besides the Ancients that we have spoke of before, *Scipio* would make the *Romans* believe that he undertook nothing without the Advice of *Jupiter Capitolinus*; *Sylla*, that all his Actions were countenanc'd by *Apollo*, of whom he always wore a small Portraicture: And *Sertorius*, that his *Fawn* brought him the News of all that was concluded in the Council of the Gods. But to come to the Histories that are nearest to our times, it is certain, that by the same Methods *James Bussularius* govern'd some time at *Pavia*, *John de Vincente* at *Bolonia*, and *Jerom Savanarola* at *Florence*; of whom we have this Remark in *Matchiavel*, (upon *Livy*) *The People of* Florence *are no Fools, and yet* Jerom Savanorala *made them believe that he spoke with God*

Almighty. It is not above threescore Years since *William Postellus* did the same in *France*, and *Campanella* not long ago in the *Upper Calabria*. But they could not compass their Ends any more than the former, because they had not a Force sufficient at their Command; for as *Matchiavel* says, This Condition is necessary to all those who would establish a new Religion. And it was in effect by that means that *Sophi Ismael* having, by the Advice of *Treschel Cuselbas*, introduc'd a new Sect among the *Mahometans*, did afterwards usurp the Empire of *Persia*. And it happen'd much about the same time that the Hermit *Schacoculis*, after having play'd his part for seven Years in the Desart, laid aside his Mask, and being declar'd Author of a new Sect, seiz'd upon several Cities, defy'd the Basha of *Anatolia*, with *Corcut* the Son of *Bajazet*; and had gone much farther, if b robbing a Caravan he had not provok'd the Sophi of *Persia* to cut him in pieces. Amongst these *Lipsius* places a certain Fortune-teller, who by a feign'd Devotion, over-run all *Natolia*, found means to employ the *Turkish* Forces, till such time as he was defeated in a pitch'd Battle: And one *Ismael* an *African*, who took his way to wrest the Kingdom from his Master the King of *Morocco*.

The second Invention that Politicians have made use of to make Religion have an Influence over the People, has been to counterfeit Miracles, feign Dreams, invent Monsters and Prodigies:

> *Quæ Vitæ rationem vertere possent,*
> *Fortunasq; omnes magno turbare timore.*

That might o'erturn the Conduct of our Lives,
And harrass all Affairs with panick Fear.

So we see that *Alexander* being inform'd by a Physician, of a sovereign Remedy for the poison'd Arrows of the Enemies, made it be thought that it was reveal'd to him in a Dream; and *Vespasian* got People, who feign'd themselves to be blind and lame, that he might cure them by his Touch. It was for this Reason, that *Clovis* accompanied his Conversion with so many Miracles; that *Charles* the VIIth advanc'd the Credit of the Maid of *Orleans*, and the present Emperor that of the Father *Jesus Maria*, in hopes perhaps of gaining a Battle equal to that of *Prague*.

The third has for its Foundation false Reports, Revelations, and Prophesies, which are spread abroad to move, frighten, and astonish the People, or to confirm, encourage, and embolden them, according as the different Occasions may require. And to this end *Postellus* tells us, that *Mahomet* had with him a famous Astrologer, who did nothing else but preach concerning a great Revolution, that was to happen both in Religion and the Empire, with a long Train of happy Successes that were to follow it, that by this means he might open the way for *Mahomet*, and prepare the People the more willingly to receive that Religion he was going to introduce; and at the same time cast a dread upon them that would not approve it, by suspecting, they should resist the Order of Destiny, by opposing this new Favourite of Heaven, since he has always the greatest Advantage:

Cui militat Æther,
Etconjurati veniunt ad classica Venti.

For whom the Heav'n declares,
Whilst the combining Winds assist his Wars.

It was the Help of such an easy Credulity, that *Ferdinando Cortez* gain'd the Kingdom of *Mexico,* where he was receiv'd as if he had been the *Topilchiu,* whose Arrival about that time had been foretold by some Prophesiers; and so *Francis Pizarro* enter'd upon the Empire of *Peru,* with the general Applause of all the People, who took him for the Person that *Vilaroca* should send to deliver their King out of Captivity. Even *Charlemagne* penetrated far into *Spain* b means of an old Image, which, according to a Prophecy, let fall a great Key that it had in its Hand: And the *Alaribes* or *Saracens* coming like an Inundation into the same Kingdom, under the Conduct of Count *Julian,* scarce met with any Opposition, because some time before there was a Painting found in an old Castle near *Toledo,* with Persons of such like Habits and Countenances, which was thought to have been laid up there by some great Prophet. And I dare affirm, as divers Historians have done, that without such Predictions *Mahomet* the Second had not so easily become Master of *Constantinople.* But what Example can be more remarkable, than that which happen'd in the Year 1613, in relation to the City of *Ascosta,* the Principal of the Island of *Magna,* which having revolted from the *Sophi* was easily reduc'd b *Arcomat* his General, by virtue of a Prophetical Tradition amongst the Citizens, *That if the Town did not surrender to* Arcomat, *it should be* Arcomated; that is, if it did not surrender to the *Destroyer*, it should be *destroy'd*; although if it would have defended it self it could not have been taken, seeing according to the Report of *Carcia ab Horto*, a *Portuguese* Physician, who had been there about thirty or forty Years before, it was five Leagues in compass, had fifty thousand Families, and yielded to the *Sophi* a standing Revenue of fifteen Million six hundred thousand Crowns. We see therefore that the Method is easy for Politicians to deceive and seduce the foolish Populace, by the usage of these Predictions, to make them fear or hope, receive or refuse whatever liest most for their Convenience.

But there is a shorter and more secure Method, which is that of making use of Preachers, and Persons that can speak well; for there is nothing but may be attain'd by that Stratagem. The Force of Eloquence, and an Harangue drest up with Art and fair Words, slides with so much Pleasure into the Ears, that one must be deaf, or more crafty than *Ulysses*, not to be charm'd with 'em. It is likewise true, that whatever the Poets have wrote concerning the Twelve Labours of *Hercules*, may be mythologiz'd by the different Effects of Eloquence, by which means he accomplish'd things of the utmost DIfficulty; and therefore the ancient *Gauls* had good Reason to represent him with a great many little Golden Chains coming out of his Mouth, and fix'd to the Ears of a Multitude of People that he drew after him. It was by this means,

> *Sylvestres Homines sacer interpresq; deorum*
> *Cædibus, & victu fædo deterruit Orpheus,*

Dictus ab hoc lenire Tygres rabidosq; Leones.
Horace.

> *Orpheus*, that Prophet, and that Holy Priest,
> Reliev'd Man's Life from Habits of the Beast,
> From bloody Slaughter, and from Food undrest;
> And thus his Voice gain'd the immortal Fame
> Of rendering Tygers mild, and Lions tame.

And thus *Philip* King of *Macedon*, one of the greatest Politicians that ever were, and who very well knew, that *Omnia summa ratione gesta fortuna etiam sequitur,* (as *Livy* says) *Fortune always accompanied that which is done with a consummate Prudence*, did not endeavour to attack the *Athenians* with warlike Preparations, since he knew he could overcome them more easily by the Eloquence of *Demosthenes*, and by such prejudicial Resolutions as they should take in their publick Councils. So *Pericles* made use of the fine Speeches of *Ephialtes* to render the same State of the *Athenians* entirely popular: And for this Reason the Ancients said, that the Orators had the same Power over the Populace, as the Winds had over the Sea. But to come to the Kingdom of *France:* Every one knows that the famous Croisade, so zealously manag'd by *Godfrey* of *Bouillon*, was encourag'd and undertaken by the Harangues and Sermons of a plain Man, call'd *Peter* the *Hermit*; as the Second was b those of St. *Bernard*. Was there ever a more wicked and abominable Murder than that of *Lewis* Duke of *Orleans*, in the Year 1407, committed by the Duke of *Burgundy?* And yet there was found out such a Person as Master *John Petit*, a Divine and great Preacher, who might palliate the Fact, and so cover and disguise it by the Sermons he made at *Notre Dame* in *Paris*, that all those who would afterwards maintain the Part of the House of *Orleans* were look'd upon as Rebels; which oblig'd them to use the same Artifice with their Enemy, and to put themselves under the Protection of that famous Man of Worth *John Gerson*, who undertook their Defence, and declar'd to the Council of *Constance*, that the Proposition maintain'd by *Petit* was Heretical and Erroneous. But as *John Petit* was the Cause of so great a Mischief under *Charles* the Sixth, he had another Brother Cordelier nam'd *Richard*, under *Charles* the Seventh, who was the Author of as much Good; for by ten Sermons, each of them six Hours long, he prevail'd with the People to throw into Fires prepar'd on purpose at the ends of the Streets, all their Cards, Tables, Table-men, Billiards, Dice, and such like Instruments of Gaming and Hazard, as were the Occasion of Oaths and Blasphemy. But this good Man was no sooner gone out of *Paris*, but that they began to despise and ridicule him, and return to their old Diversions with greater Application than formerly. Just in the same manner as those strange Changes or Conversions, almost miraculous, which the *Capuchin* Father *Giacinto da Casale* about twenty Years ago perform'd throughout *Italy*, by his Preaching, continu'd no longer than whilst that Father executed the Functions of that Charge. If we descend to the Time of *Francis* the First, we shall find that the Battle of *Marignan*, which was fought with so much Obstinacy by the *Switzers*, that it continu'd two whole Days together, till they were almost all slain upon the Spot, had nothing else to press them forward, but the Harangue made them by the Cardinal of *Sion*, or, as *Paulus Jovius* calls him in his

Eulogies, *Sedunensis Antistes:* For they had no sooner heard him, but they resolv'd to give Battle, and contested the Victory to the last Drop of their Blood. We shall see likewise how *Monluc*, Bishop of *Valence*, was sent to the *Venetians*, to justify by his fair Speeches the Request for *Turkish* Succours against the Emperor *Charles* the Fifth; and after the Massacre of St. *Bartholomew*, the same *Monluc* and *Pybrac* exercis'd both their Tongues and Pens to keep the *Polanders*, although fully inform'd of that Barbarity by the *Calvinists*, as has been observ'd before, from making that as an Occasion against chusing *Henry* the Third for their King. It was equally remarkable, that the first Siege of *Rochell* was better sustain'd by the continual Preaching of forty Ministers that had fled into it, than by all the Captains and Soldiers, with which it was sufficiently provided. And at the time that the *Parisians* eat Dogs and Rats rather than obey an Heretick Prince, was it not *Boucher, Rose, Wincester*, and several other Parish Priests, that kept them up in their Resolution. It is certain, that if the Protestant Minister *Chamier* had not been taken off from the Bastions of *Montauban* by a Cannon-Ball, that Town might been as difficult to have been taken as *Rochelle*. And when *Campanella* had a Design of making himself King of the *Upper Calabria*, he chose out for his Companion one *Denis Pontius*, a Fryar, who had gain'd the Reputation of one of the most eloquent and persuasive Persons of that Age. Let us look into the Old Testament, which God would deliver to his People by his Servant *Moses*, who was not so proper to command, because he was a Man slow of Speech, and of a few Words; he therefore bad him make use of the Eloquence of his Brother *Aaron*, Exod.

4. 14. Is not Aaron *the* Levite *ty Brother? I know that he can speak well. And though shalt speak unto him, and put Words in his Mouth.* And afterwards, *ch. 7. v.* I. *See I have made thee a God to* Pharaoh, *and* Aaron *thy Brother shall be thy Prophet. Thou shalt speak all that I command thee, and thy Brother shall speak unto* Pharaoh. This is what the Pagans, the Apes of our Mysteries, would afterwards represent by their *Pallas*, the Goddess of Eloquence, who was arm'd with a Lance, a Buckler, and Helmet, to shew that Arms can make but small Progress without Eloquence, nor Eloquence without Arms. Now seeing these two different Qualities seldom join and accompany one another in the same Person, as *Virgil* has well observ'd in the Character of *Drances; Cui Lingua melior, sed frigida bello dextera*, whose Tongue was prevalent, but his Arm feeble. The greatest Captains have for this Reason, to supply this Defect, always taken with them, and contracted a Friendship with some Person, who was able by the Efforts of his Speech to second those of their Swords: *Ninus*, for Example, to this purpose made use of *Zoroaster*, *Agamemnon* of *Nestor*, *Diomedes* of *Ulysses*, *Pyrrhus* of *Cyneas*, *Trajan* of *Pliny the Younger*, *Theodoric* of *Cassiodorus*. And the same may be said of all the great Warriors, who have caress'd this *Venus Verticordia, the Goddess who can change and turn the Heart as she pleases,* no less than the former, as being ignorant that

> *Cultus habet Sermo & supiens mirabile robur,*
> *Imperat Affectus varios, Animumq; gubernat.*

Smooth and wise Speech does bear a wondrous
Force,
Governs the Passions, and commands the Mind.

It is my own Opinion, That Eloquence is so powerful, that nothing hitherto has been exempt from its Empire: It is that which makes the most fabulous Religions obtain Belief, that raises the most unjust Wars, conceals or gives false Colours to the blackest Actions, which calms and appeases the most violent Seditions, which stirs the most peaceable Tempers to Rage and Fury; in short, it is that which plants and roots out Heresies, that made *England* revolt, and converted *Japan*,

Limus ut hic durescit & hæc ut certa liquescit.
Uno eodemque igne.   Virgil. Eclog.

as the same Fire hardens the Clay, and melts the Wax; and if a Prince had twelve Men of such Parts at his Devotion, I should esteem him stronger, and that he could command more Obedience in his Country, than if he had two powerful Armies. But since Eloquence may be made use of after two manners, both in speaking and writing, it may be remark'd that the second is not of less Consequence than the first, and I dare say, that upon some Accounts it surpasses it; for a Man that speaks cannot be heard but in one place, and by three or four thousand Men at once.

Gaude quod videant oculi te mille loquentem.

——You're pleas'd to think

A thousand Eyes gaze on you while you speak.

Whereas he that writes may declare his thoughts in all Places, and to all Persons. I may add, that many prevalent Reasons often escape the Ears thro' the Precipitation of the Tongue, which cannot so easily deceive the Eyes, when the same thing may at leisure be viewed by them; what Weapons can't obtain, has been often gain'd by a single Declaration or Manifesto. Therefore *Francis* the First, and *Charles* the Fifth, manag'd their Wars as much by Letters and Apologies, as by their Swords and Launces; and we find in our time, that the Quarrel between the Pope and the *Venetians*, the Oath of Allegiance in *England*, the Favour of the Marquis *d'Ancre*, and Messieurs *de Luyne* in *France*, the War of the *Palatinate* in *Germany*, and the *Valtolin* in *Switzerland*, have produc'd an infinite number of Pamphlets, as well prejudicial to one side, as favourable to the other. They who have seen the marvellous Effects which *Cassandra*, and the Ghost of *Henry the Great* produc'd against the Marquis *d'Ancre*, the *Conradin Provençal*, and the *Hermit* of *Mount Valerian* against *Messieurs de Luyne*; *le Mot a l'Oreille, & la Voix publique*, or *The Word in the Ear*, or *the Publick Voice*, against the Marquis *de la Veiuville*; the *Admonition*, or *Mysteria Politica*, or *Political Mysteries* of *Jansenius* against our King, cannot doubt, I think, what weight such sort of Writings bear along with them. And God grant that they which are daily sent from *Brussels*, may not have as much against the present State of *France*, or that Persons may be found as capable and hearty to defend the King's Interest vigorously against the disaffected Party, as Father *Paul* was in the Cause of the

Venetians, and *Pibrac* and *Monluc* in that of *Charles* the Ninth, and *Henry* the Third, against the furious Calumnies of all the *Calvinists.*

But after having fully discours'd of all the Means to accommodate Religion to Politick Affairs, that must not be forgot which has always been most us'd, and put in practice with the greatest Subtlety, which is the undertaking of a thing under the pretence of Religion, that nothing else could render prevalent or lawful; and in effect, the Proverb commonly used by the *Jews, In nomine Domini committitur omne malum,* that in the Name of God all Evil is committed, is not less true than the Reproach that Pope *Leo* made to the Emperor *Theodosius.* "*Privatæ Causæ pietatis aguntur obtentu, & cupiditatum quisque suarum Religionem habet Pedissequam.* Private Affairs are transacted under the Cloak of Piety, and every one makes Religion the Handmaid of his own Desires." But since Examples are so common that all Books are full of them, I shall content my self, having spoken of the *French* already, with mentioning some of the *Spanish* ones, and following punctually what *Mariana,* the most faithful of their Historians has observ'd concerning them. Speaking then of the Ancient *Goths* who reign'd in *Spain,* and of the Wars that they made to drive out one another; he says they made use of Religion as their Pretence to Dominion; so when King *Josenand* call'd the *Burgundians,* who were *Arians,* to his Assistance, in driving out King *Svintila,* his Expression is, *Optimum fore judicavit religionis prætextum,* Book 6. ch. 5. He judg'd that his best Method would be the pretence of Religion, and describing how *Eringius* drove out King

Wamba, Optimum visum est religionis speciem pretendere, Chap. 7. Religion was to be the specious Excuse of it, and when two Brothers of the House of *Aragon, Violento imperiosi Pontificis mandato*, By the violent Command of that imperious Pope *Boniface* the Eighth, took Arms against one another; this good Father very pertinently observes, that nothing was more in human than such a Violation of the Laws of Nature, *Sed tanti Fide Religioque fuere*, but of such value to them were their Faith and Religion, *Book* 5. c. 2. And speaking of *Navarre,* which *Ferdinand, immensa imperandi ambitione,* through an immense Ambition of Empire, took away from his own Niece, he adds for excuse, *Sed species Religionis prætexta facto est & Pontificis jussa*, but Religion and the Pope's Commands were the specious Pretences for this Fact, *Book* 25. *Ch. ult.* In short, not to alledge all that this fine Author has remark'd, I shall refer to the Book it self, which is full of nothing else, and passing to *Charles* the First, I shall produce what *Francis* the First says against him in his Apology of the Year 1537. *Charles vint empieter sur les Estats sous Couleur de Religion*, That *Charles* would gain footing in all Countries, under the Colour of Religion. And speaking of the War of *Germany, L'Empereur sous Couleur de Religion armé de la ligue des Catholiques, veut opprimer l'autre & se faire le chemin a la Monarchie.* That the Emperor, under Colour of Religion, arm'd with a Catholick League, would oppress the other Party, and make a way to the Universal Monarchy, which likewise was very well remark'd by Monsieur *de Nevers*, in the Passage that we have cited before. Lastly, when the late King *James* was called to the Crown of *England*, the King of *Spain* made haste to enter into a strict Band of Alliance with him; the Constable of *Castile* was sent thither, a Relation of it was printed, and *Rovida*, Senator of *Milan*, calls this Alliance a very sanctified Work, and acknowledges the King of England for a very Holy Christian Prince, offers him in his Master's Name all the Spanish Forces by Sea and Land, and protests that the King of *Spain* did it *Divina Admonitione, Divina Voluntate, Divine Ope, non nisi magno Dei Beneficio*, by the Divine Admonition, by the Divine Will, by the Divine Assistance, by God's great Bounty. Since therefore it is natural to most Princes to treat Religion like Mountebanks, and use it as a Drug to maintain the Credit and Reputation of their Stage, one ought not in any Opinion to blame a Politician, if to accomplish some important Affair, he have recourse to the same Industry, though it be more decent to say the contrary, and indeed to speak rightly.

> *Non sunt hæc dicenda palam prodendaque vulgo,*
> *Quippe hominum prelique mali, plerique scelesti.*
> Palingenius in Libra.

> This from the Vulgar should be hidden still,
> They are already vers'd enough in ill.

However, all these Maxims would remain without due Regard and Splendor, if they were not heightned, and as it were animated by another, which teaches us to give them their right Byass, and *make a good Choice of the Hour and Time favourable for the putting them in execution, lest otherwise if that be neglected they may do as much Mischief.*

Besides, it is not sufficient to have acquir'd that Prudence which is ordinary and common to Statesmen, if we do not proceed to another more refin'd, and which is only proper to the most subtle and experienc'd Politicians to know the value of fortuitous Occasions, and to draw Profit and Advantage from that which would have been neglected by another, or perhaps have redounded to his Prejudice. Such was that great Eclipse which happen'd under the Emperor *Tiberius*, when all the Legions in *Hungary* had mutiny'd to that degree, that there seem'd to be no appearance of their being appeas'd; for a Person less refin'd than *Drusus* would have neglected this Occasion, and never have thought of gathering any Profit from it; but he, seeing that the Mutineers were in a great Consternation upon this sudden Darkness, because they did not know the Reason of it, fell upon the Horse, surpriz'd, and struck such a Terror in them, that by this Accident he brought that to pass, which all other Generals, and he himself would otherwise have despair'd to have effected. Such was likewise the Stratagem with which King *Tullus* ingeniously us'd to cover the Revolt of *Metius Suffetius*, and drew thence an uncommon Advantage by causing the Word to pass from Squadron to Squadron, that he had sent him to surprize the Enemies, and cut off all hopes of their Retreat. I much wonder therefore how *Titus Livius*, and *Cornelius Tacitus*, who relate these Stories, are content to draw thence only particular Conclusions, and that the first should say no more than that *Stratagema est, quæ in certamine a transfugis nostris perfide fiunt, ea dicere fieri nostro jussu,* It is a Stratagem to say, that what Deserters do in a Battel, is done by our own Appointment. And the other, *In commoto populo sedando, convertenda in sapientiam & occasionem mitigationis quæ casus obtuli, & quæ populus ille pavet aut observat supersitiose:* In appeasing the Commotions of a People, those things are to be converted to Prudcence, and a Handle taken thence to appease them, which Chance offers,and which that People fears or observes with Superstition, without drawing thence this general Maxim, *Quæ casus obtulit in sapientiam vertenda,* What Chance offers is to be converted to Prudence; since not only Treasons and Mutinies, but other matters may be turn'd to that use: So *Columbus* having observ'd the Time in which a great Eclipse should happen, he threatned the Inhabitants of the new World, that he would turn the Moon into Blood, and take it entirely away from them, unless they furnish'd him with the Provisions he had occasion for, which were immediately sent him as soon as the Eclipse began to appear. I have remark'd before, that *Ferdinando Cortez* made the Inhabitants of *Mexico* believe that he was the God *Topilchin,* that he might the more easily get Possession of their Kingdom, and that *Francis Pizarro* us'd the same Stratagem in the Conquest of *Peru;* by calling himself the *Viracoca.* It was by this Method that *Mahomet* chang'd his Epilepsie into an Extasie; and *Charles* the Fifth made use of the Heresie of *Luther,* to weaken the Princes of *Germany,* who being united, might have control'd the Authority he would acquire in the Empire, and hinder the Project he had contrived for an Universal Monarchy. We may say farther, that the same Emperor not having Spirit and Judgment strong enough to govern such large Dominions as he was Master of, and seeing that the growing Fortune of *Henry* the Second put Bounds to his, and that he made a Jest of the Motto of *Plus ultra*, farther still, and gave occasion to the Pasquinades to jingle upon *Metæ*, the Latin Name of the City *Met*, and the Latin Word *Meta* signifying a Boundary, as if that City was the farthest Place he could go to,

Sifte pedem Metis, hæc tibi meta datur.

He cover'd all thees Disgraces under the Veil of Piety and Religion, shutting up himself in a Cloyster, where he had likewise the opportunity of repenting of the secret Sins which he had committed, by getting a Bastard Son that was his Nephew: So *Philip* the Second took occasion to vacate the Privileges of the *Aragonians*, upon their affording Protection to *Antonio Perez*; and I find amongst our Kings of *France*, that *Philip* the First very much enlarged his Kingdom, and deliver'd himself from the Guardianship (if it may be so call'd) of the Majors of the Palace, whilst all the Princes of *France* and his Brother were busie fighting against the *Saracens*, under the Conduct of *Godfrey of Bulloin*. And it may be said, that during the said Crusade, *Philip the August* abandon'd *Richard* King of *England*, that he might return into *France,* to embroil the Affairs of the English; because in Matters of State, *Quædam nisi, fallacia vires assimpserint, fidem propositi non inveniunt laudemque occulto magis tramite, quam via recta petunt;* There are some Things that don't give Credit to their Proposal, unless they gather Strength from some Fallacy, and seek for Praise rather in some secret Way, than in the direct Road.

CHAP. V. *What Conditions are requisite to a Minister, with whom such Master Strokes of State may be concerted.*

HERE it may be objected to me, that I ought not to treat of the Qualities of a Minister, until I have spoken of those of the Prince, since it is he that gives the first Spring and Motion to all that is done in the Council, as the *Primum Mobile* draws all the other Heavens along with it, and the Sun communicates its Light to the Stars and Planets: But to this I answer, that Sovereigns are plac'd over us by Succession or Election; now of these two means, the first follows Nature, to which we punctually pay Obedience, without Restriction, or the Consideration of any Circumstance.

Dum pecudes auro dum murice vestit Asellos.

Whilst the brute Ass in Gold and Purple brays.

And the second tuns upon Intriegue, Self-Interest, and the Cabals of such Persons as are most rich and most powerful in Friends, Favours, and ready Money to satisfie their Ambition; so that it would be like a Pedant to propose, or even to think that the Consideration of a Virtue or Merit can have any place amidst such a Disorder. But as to what relates to Ministers, one may Philosophize after another manner; because the depend absolutely upon the Choice that the Prince may make of them, that being permitted him, nay even decent and honourable, for him to take from amongst all his Friends and Domesticks, that Person that he thinks best qualify'd for the Employment in which he will place him, *Sapientissimum enim dicunt eum esse cui quod opus fit veniet in mentem; proxime accedere eum qui alterius bene inventis obtemperet.* (Cicero *for* Cluentius) "He is said to be the wisest Man that can conceive in his own Mind those things that he has need of; and he approaches next to him that can condescend to the good Intentions of another Person." I add farther, that besides the Honour a Prince acquires by such a Choice, he does from thence likewise gather a very great Profit, and so considerable, that if he will not neglect and abandon himself, he will be almost under a necessity to proceed to such a Choice. *Velleius Paterculus* has very well observ'd to this purpose, that *Magna Negotia magnis Adjutoribus egent,* (Book 2.) Great Affairs require great Assistants; and *Tacitus* says that *Gravissimi Principis laboris queis orbem Terræ capessit, egent adminiculis,* (12 Annals.) The heavy Labours of a Prince, who governs the Globe of Earth wants Supporters, to which may be added that excellent Saying of *Euripides,*

Σοφος τύραννος τῶν σοφῶν συνθεσία, *A Prince becomes wise by the Conversation of wise Men.* And indeed Histories teach us that they have always been esteemed the wisest Princes, who have done nothing of their own Heads, and without the Advice of some faithful and trusty Minister, from whence *Alexander* had always near him his *Clitus* and *Hephestion*; *Augustus* did nothing without the Advice of *Mecænas* and *Agrippa*; that *Nero* was the best of Emperors whilst he follow'd the Counsels of *Burrbus* and *Seneca*; and to come nearer to our own Knowledge, *Charles* the Fifth, and *Philip* the Second had *de Chevres*, and *Ruy de Gomez* for their Assistants, as likewise the intimate Councellors of *Charles* the Eighth were at several times, the Count *de Dunois, Louvet* President of *Provence, Tannegui du Chastel*, and the Count *de Dammarttin*. As for what relates to his Son *Lewis* the Eleventh, as he was always dissident, variable and restless in his Temper, so he often chang'd his secret Servants and Confidents, but still he had some one to whom he would communicate his Mind more freely than to others; as to the Cardinal *Ballue, Philip de Comines*, and *Cottier* his Physican. *Charles* the Eighth did the same to Cardinal *Brissonet*, and his Successor *Lewis* the Twelfth to Cardinal *d'Amboise*, who possess'd him entirely. King *Francis* the First put more Confidence in Admiral *Annibant* than in any other Person, and *Henry* the Second, in the Constable *Montmorency*. In short, we see in the Course of our Annals, that the two Brothers of the House of *Lorrain* were the Support of *Francis* the Second, the Cardinal *Birague* of *Charles* the Ninth, Monsieur *Espernon* of *Henry* the Third, Messieurs *de Sully, Villeroy* and *Sillery* of *Henry* the Fourth, and Monseigneur the Cardinal of *Richelieu* of our King *Louis* the *Just* and the *Triumphant*.

But this Maxim being establish'd as most true and certain, that Princes ought to have some secret and trusty Counsellor, the Politicians are in difficulty to resolve whether he ought to be contented with one alone, or to have many in an equal and the like degree of Confidence; for if one would act by Reasons and Examples, *Xenophon* on the one side advises, that Πολλοί βασιλέως όφθαλμοί κ, πολλά ὦτα, (Book 13. Cyropæd.) *A King should have many Eyes and many Ears,* and the Triumvirat which so happily govern'd *France* under *Henry* the *Fourth,* would make good the Saying, though we had not the Example of *Augustus* and the Ancients. On the other side, we know that amongst divers Persons, *Non voto vivitur uno,* there cannot be the same desire, and that in Affairs nothing is more prejudicial or troublesome than the diversity of Opinions; that Hatred, Ambition, Vain-Glory, and such like Passions make them often propose and authorise what is directly contrary to Reason. And *Tacitus* has very properly remark'd, *Cæde Messalina convulsa est Cæsaris Domus, orto apud Libertos Certamine*; That when *Messalina* was slain *Cæsar*'s Family was shock'd by the Contests that arose amongst the Freemen; for as a great number of Physicians are often destructive to the Patient, so too a great number of Counsellors almost always ruin the Affairs that are under their Consideration. It seems therefore necessary to bring two so different Opinions to some Agreement, to use this distinction, That if a Prince knows himself to have Strength, Authority, Judgment and Capacity enough to be above his Councellors and Confidents, it will be well for him to have three or four, because that after they have delivered their Opinion upon any incident, he may draw many Inferences and Conclusions from them all, and at last put that in Execution which he shall most esteem expedient. But if he is of a weak Spirit, and not of a Capacity large enough to chuse the best Advice and put it in practice, it is without doubt more expedient that he shall make Choice of as the most judicious and best qualified of all of them; because if he commits himself to more of them, it may happen that each may have his different and particular Interest, his different Intentions and Designs, upon which the Prince not being able to regulate them and to make use of the principal Intrigues and Parties which will be form'd in his Council, Ambition will be prevalent, and so will Jealousy, which follows it as close as it does Love; Reason will do nothing, but Passion do all; Secrecy will be banish'd, and whilst the poor Prince is thus strangely disquieted, he will not be able to resolve on the one side or the other, but will furnish Discourse for his People and Sport for his Ministers. This has been judiciously remark'd by *Tacitus*, in relation to the Emperor *Galba, Quippe hiantes in magna fortuna amicorum cupiditates ipsa Galbæ facilitas intendebat; cum apud infirmum & credulum minori metu & majori præmio percaretur*, That the too great easiness of *Galba* increas'd the Covetousness of his Friends; for Faults might be committed with less Fear and greater Reward, when they met with a weak and credulous Temper. The like happen'd to the Emperor *Claudius*, and in our Time to *Charles* the *Eighth*, in the Affairs relating to *Pisa* and *Siena*. *Guicciardine* makes the same Observation concerning *Clement* the *Eighth*, and the *Italian* Politicians from thence have fram'd this Maxim, *Ogni Volta che un Principe fara in mano di piu quando non habbia consiglio e prudenza da se, sara preda da Tutti*, Whenever a Prince is in the Hands of many, if he has not Council and Prudence in himself, he becomes a Prey to all of them: Whereas on the contrary, if he confides in one Minister well qualified, and us'd with that regard that a Master ought to have for a faithful

Servant, all things will go better for the Prince, his Credit will be preserv'd to him, his Authority maintain'd, his Person belov'd, his Commands executed, and his whole Country will feel the like Effects to those which *France* at present receives from the wise Government of Cardinal *Richelieu*.

This then being granted, that a Prince ought to have a Minister or Counsellor who is secret, faithful, and that may be confided in, we ma now see how he ought to chuse him, and what Qualities he should be endow'd with; or to speak more exactly, what should be the Properties both of his Body and the Accidents that attend it, as likewise of his Mind. After which we shall add what a Prince ought to contribute to the satisfaction of his Minister, and so put an end to the present Discourse.

Now as to the first Point, which is to show, of what Quality, Office, or sort of Person a Minister is to be chosen, I shall find my self as much embarrass'd as *Vegetius* was to resolve from what Place or sorts of Men one might chuse a good Soldier: For as all Affairs are not alike, so all sorts of Persons are not always proper for the diversity of Negotiations, no more than every sort of Wood was heretofore fitting to make an Image of *Mercury*. However to solve this difference we must distinguish between a Minister that is to give Counsel, and a Minister that is to put it in execution; for although both of them ought to take this Advice from *Livy* (Book 24.) *Magis nullius interest quam tua* T. Otacili, *non imponi cervicibus tuis onus sub quo concidas*, It is your Interest, *Titus Otacilius*, to see that the Burden laid upon your Shoulders be not such as you must sink under: Yet each of them must be consider'd in particular, and must have different Properties. As to what concerns the latter, he should be taken from amongst the most noble and illustrious Families, that he may exercise his Charge and Command with the greater Splendor, Grandeur and Authority; care should be likewise taken that he has an Inclination and Sufficiency proportionable to the Employment for which he is design'd,

Nec enim loricam possit Achilles, Thersites.

For *Thersites* can lay no Claim to the Armor of *Achilles*. And as *Appius* was not able to govern the Populace, *Cleon* did not understand the Conduct of an Army; *Philopæmen* knew not how to command at Sea; *Pericles* was fit to Govern, *Diomedes* to Fight, *Ulysses* to Counsel. Advantages ought to be drawn from these different Inclinations, that when a Vacancy happens he may be call'd to supply it, who by his natural Genius can exercise it with the greatest Honour and Satisfaction; otherwise Wrong would be done, if they who are born to Command, should be subjected to such as are fram'd only to obey; should the Command of an Army be given to a Person that has neither Experience nor Courage, or an Embassy be committed to one that has neither Presence nor Utterance. It being much more proper, as an ancient Author advises, *Quemque cuique Functioni pro indole admovere*, To prefer every Person according to their Capacity. But as to the choice of a secret Minister the case is otherwise, and to resolve the Doubt propos'd, whether he ought to be taken from one of the most illustrious

Families, or from amongst Persons of a lower Station; it seems may be done from both of them indifferently, *Dum nullum fastidiretur genus in quo eniteret virtus, crevit Imperium Romanum.* (Livy. *Book* 4.) The *Roman* Empire was enlarg'd by not disdaining to make use of the Service of Persons of any Condition, provided they were eminent for their Virtue. There are however these difficulties in regard to great Lords and Nobles, that they are Envious of others, that often instead of obeying they will command, that they Counsel the Prince rather for their own particular Interest, than the good of the State; that they will advance their Creatures and ruin those who are not of their Cabal; that they will often encroach upon the Authority of their Masters, as the Majors of the Palace did in *France*, who embroil'd the Kingdom to make themselves necessary; that they are never content with what is given them, as being below what they think they have deserv'd, both for their Services and the Grandeur of their Family. In short it seems to me upon this Occasion, where the Nobility and Dignity of the Persons are not of so much Use as their Advice, Counsel and Judgment. A Marquis or Prince may not succeed better than Men of meaner Condition, and yet cause a great deal of Mischief; whereas these on the contrary may do as good, are not so chargeable, are more obedient, easy and tractable, and have not so much to be apprehended from them. And indeed *Seneca* in his Epistles had reason to say, *Nulli præclusa est virtus omnes admittit, nec censum nec sexum eligit,* Virtue is not inaccessible to any Person, admits every one without distinction of Estates or Sexes. From whence *Tacitus* has remark'd, that the *Germans* call'd even their Wives to Council, *Nec Concilia earum aspernebantur nec responsa negligebant*, Nor was their Advice despis'd or their Decisions neglected. *Plutarch* affirms the same of the *Lacedæmonians*, and many Historians relate it of *Augustus*, and *Justinian*. And *Cæcilius* says very right in *Cicero's Tusculan* Questions, *Sæpe etiam sub surdido pallio latet Sapientia*, Wisdom often lies hid under a mean Habit. It is Opportunity, Employment, and Business which discovers it, and makes it shine forth with Lustre. If *Matthew Paunier* the *Florentin*, had not been employ'd in the Embassy to King *Alphonso* where he acquitted himself so handsomely, he would have been thought fit for nothing else but pounding in the Mortar, and making up Clysters. If Cardinal *d'Ossat* had not been sent to manage Affairs in the Court of *Rome*, he would have been thought only fit to play the Pedant in the College of *Paris*, and to defend *Ramus* against *Charpentier*. And the like may be said of the Cardinals *Balue, Ximenes* and *Perron, Quorum Nobilitas sola fuit atque unica Virtus*, Who had no other Nobility but their Virtue. And why may not Men of good Spirits proceed from out of all sorts of Conditions. *Cardan* was a Physician, *Bodin* an Advocate, *Charron* a Divine, *Montagne* a Gentleman, *La Noüe* a Soldier, and Father *Paul* a Monk.

Sæpe etiam est Olitor verba opportuna locutus.

Often the Peasant does in Season speak.

Therefore it is that I exclude no Person from this Charge, not even *Strangers* themselves; because *Tiberius, Subinde res suas quibusdam ignotis mandabat*, Sometimes committed the Administration of his Affairs to unknown sort of Persons. (*Tacit.* Annals Book 4.) And *Charles* the *Fifth* made use of *Granvelle, Francis,* the *First* of *Trivulse, Henry* the *Second* of *Strozzi, and Charles* the *Ninth* of Cardinal *de Briague.* Note, even *young People,* because *cani indices ætatis non sapientiæ,* grey Hairs are the marks of Age and not of Wisdom. And *Cicero* (in the fifth *Philippick*) tells us, *Ab eximia Virtute progressum ætatis expectari non non oportere,* That an extraordinary Virtue does not always wait for Age: Of which we have Examples in *Joseph, David, Ephestion* and *Papyrius: Nor yet* old Men, *because that* Moses, *by the Advice of Jethro* his Father-in-Law, chose seventy Elders to assist in the Government of the People of *Israel*; and that *Lewis* the *Eleventh* had like to have been overwhelm'd with a Civil War, because he would not confide in the old Counsellors that had been left him by his Father. Not the *Unlearned,* because as *Seneca* sas, *Paucis ad bonam mentem opus est literis,* A sound Mind has occasion for but little Learning; and that according to the Opinion of *Thucydides,* the grosser Spirits are more proper to govern the People than those which are more subtle and refin'd; great Wits having this Property, that they are more inclinable to innovate than to manage Affairs, *Novandis quam gerendis rebus aptiora* (*Curtius* Book 3.) to dissipate than preserve, to pursue their Point with obstinacy, than to yield and accommodate themselves to the Necessity of Affairs, and seems to treat with Angels and Intelligences rather than with Men. *Qhod enim celeriter arripiunt id quum tarde percipi vident discruciantur,* (*Cicero* for *Roscius*) For they are griev'd to see that go on slowly which they have enterpriz'd with precipitation. Not the *learned,* because *Imperator* Alexander *Concilios toga & Militiæ literatos adbibebat, & maxime eos qui Historiam norûnt.* (*Lampridius* in his Life). The Emperor *Alexander* made use of learned Men in his Councils, Civil and Military, and of such especially as were skilful in History: And that Cardinal *Richelieu* was taken out of his Library to the Government of *France.* Not *Philosophers*, because of *Xenophon, Seneca*, and *Plato.* Not *Physicians*, because *Oribasus* by his good Counsel had Advice rais'd *Julian* to the Empire. That *Apollophanes* was the chief of *ANtiochus* his Council; that *Stephen* was sent by the Emperor *Justinian* to *Cofroes*; that *James Cottier* and *Oliver le Dain* were the principal Councellors of *Lewis* the Eleventh, as the Father of Monsieur the Chancellor *l'Hospital* was of *Charles de Bourbon*, and Monsieur *de Miron* of *Henry* the Third. Not *Monastick Persons*, because of Father *Paul* of *Venice:* Nor to conclude, *any other* sort of Persons whatsoever, provided that it is with the Conditions and Qualifications which we shall explain hereafter. *Magna enim ingenia sæpe in occulto latent,* The greatest Wits lie hid under the greatest Secrecy, as *Plautus* says. And Prudence and Wisdom don't make choice of Personages, they dwell in the Tub of *Diogenes* as well as the Schools, under the Cowl and threadbare Clothes, as well as amongst the delicacies and sumptuousness of Pallaces. So true is it, that *Nescio quomodo factum est ut semper bonæ mentis soror sit paupertas,* It happens after an unaccountable manner, that Poverty and a sound Mind should be related in so near a degree as that of Sisters.

Now the Qualifications which a Minister ought to bring and contribute to the Service of his Prince, cannot be sufficiently explain'd without difficulty. It is that which has put Writers to so much Trouble, that which has open'd a Field for so much Discourse, and produc'd such a Multitude of Books upon the Idea, the Example, and the perfect Description of a good Councellor, of a prudent Politician and a Statesman; though all these Authors rather resemble the Archers of *Diogenes*, which shoot beyond the Mark, than to *Cicero* in his Book of the *Orator*, or *Xenophon* in his *Prince.* As for my self, who have not undertaken as they have done, to publish a large Book of all the VIrtues under the Umbrage of three or four, which are necessary to a Minister. I shall say first, I would have a Minister such in effect as he is reputed to be, that he be known to the Prince, and chosen by himself out of the Consideration of his Merits, without any other Recommendation than that of his own Virtue: *Virtute enim ambire oportet non favotoribus.* Many People who come upon the Theatre of the World, to enter into Places of Trust and Honour, appear clothed with borrow'd Ornaments, Favours, Friends, Money, Sollicitations, and ambitious Pursuits. They represent *Æsop*'s Crow adorn'd with the Feathers of other Birds, and make a Show with what is not their own, to obtain that which they don't deserve; but their Nakedness appears in despite of all their clothing, and they expose themselves to Shame upon the Theatre which they design'd for their Glory. It is necessary therefore that a Man who would preserve himself in Credit and Reputation to the Conclusion, to enter and penetrate into the good Opinion of his Master, adorn'd with Garments of his own making, that is to say, of Prudence, Virtue, Merit, Courage, and in short, of such things as are his own Growth. It is necessary that as the Sun he should produce the Light from within, by which he shines upon that which is abroad, for fear lest he should resemble the Moon, which appear only by a borrow'd Light, he should quickly show his Failures. But because there is nothing to be spoke of Merit in general, unless we determine in particular what are the Virtues which compose them, I believe they may all be refer'd to three principal ones, that is, Fortitude, Justice and Prudence; upon which I will enlarge my self a little, to explain them after a less trivial and common manner than that of the Schools.

By Fortitude I understand that temper and disposition of Spirit always equal in it self, Firm, Stable, Heroick, capable of seeing, hearing and doing every thing without being disturb'd, undone and amaz'd; which Virtue may be easily acquir'd by continual reflections upon the Condition of our Nature which is feeble, frail, and subject to all sorts of Sickness and Infirmity; upon the Vanity of the Pomps and Honours of this World, upon the Weakness and Failures of our Spirits, upon the Changes and Revolutions of Affairs, upon the various Phases and Positions of the Heavens and the Earth, upon the diversity of Opinions, Sects and Religions, upon the short Duration of every thing; in brief upon the great Advantages that arise from the avoidance of Vice and pursuit of Virtue. It comes near to that which *Juvenal* describes in these beautiful Verses of his tenth Satyr.

> *Fortem posce animum mortis terrore vacantem*
> *Quis spatium vitæ extremum inter munera ponat*

Naturæ, qui ferre queat quoscund; dolores
Nesciat irasci; cupiat nihil; & potiores
Herculis ærumnas ducat sævosq, labores
Et venere & plumis & cænis Sardanapali.

Forgive the Gods the rest, and stand confin'd
To Health of Body and Content of Mind,
A Soul that can securely Death defy,
And count it Nature's Privilege to die;
Serene and manly, harden'd to sustain,
The Load of Life, and exercis'd in pain;
Guiltless of Hate and Proof against Desire;
That all things weighs and nothing can admire;
That dares prefer the Toils of *Hercules*
To Dalliance, Banquets and ignoble Ease.
Mr. Dryden's Juvenal.

Monsieur the Chancellor *de l'Hospital*, who possess'd as much of this Fortitude of Mind as any of them who went before or follow'd after him, describes it in fewer Words, but bolder, from whence he compos'd his Device, *Si fractus illabatur orbis Impavidum ferient ruinæ*, Though the Fabrick of the World should be broken, the Ruins might strike but not frighten him. But after this Ministry there were so many feeble and effeminate Spirits, so many cowardly and mean Souls that they were frightned at the approach of Difficulties, that they fled from the least Resistance, and lost their Wits when mention was made of any great Resolution. I would have him have the Soul of *Epictetus, Socrates, Epicurus, Seneca, Brutus, Cato,* or to make use of more modern and familiar Examples, of Father

Paul, of Cardinal *d'Ossat*, of the President *Jannin*, of your *Eminence*, of *Ferrier*, and others of the same Character. I would have him have the true Maxims of Philosophy in his Head and not only in his Books; that he should know Nature through its whole extent, and not only in part; that he should live in the World as if he were out of it, and beneath the Skies as if he were above them, not being apprehensive, as the *Gauls* were, that they should tumble on them. I would have him imagine that the Court is the place of the World where the most foolish things are said and done, where Friendships are the most whimsical, and interested, Men the most disguis'd, Masters the least affectionate to their Servants, and Fortune the most blind and foolish; that he may not upon a sudden Disgust be scandaliz'd at these Extravagancies. I would have him look upon Riches *oculo irretorto*, and when they pass by him to other Persons less deserving than himself, not to cast a repining Eye after them; that delights himself in a generous Poverty, a resoluteness in what is good, a philosophical Liberty, but such as has good Manners; that it be by Chance that he comes abroad into the World; that he lends himself to the Court and to the Service of a Master only, that he may acquit himself honestly. Now whoever shall have this first universal and general Disposition which leads a Man to an Apathy, Freedom and good Nature, will by the same means be possessed of Fidelity, *Optimum enim quemque fidelissimum puto*, For the best Man will be always the most faithful, said *Pliny* to the Emperor *Trajan.* And this faithfulness will not be common, circumscrib'd with certain Circumstances subject to several Considerations of private Interest, Persons, and the Consequences of Affairs, but such a one as a brave Man ought to be endow'd with to serve him that he is engag'd to, against all, without Exception of Place, Time or Persons. So it was that *Caius Blosius* ser'vd his Friend *Tiberius Gracchus, (Valer. Maxim.* Book 4. c. 7.) And the Father of the Chancellour *de l'Hospital* acted with *Charles* of *Bourbon*; for being his Physician and Confident in the time of his Disgrace and Persecution, he never abandon'd him, following him in a Disguise, partaking in all his Misfortunes, assisting him in all his Designs against the King, the Emperor, *Rome*, the Cardinals, and the Pope himself. An Action which his Son the great Chancellor of *France* regarded so much, that he plac'd it at the Beginning of his Will as the most remarkable one of his Family. An accomplish'd Minister therefore ought in the first place to be furnish'd with Fidelity, and when he has occasion to shew it should say,

> *Huic ego nec rerum metas nec tempora pono*
> *Obsequium sine sine dedi.*

> Not Time or Bounds my Duty shall controul,
> Beyond such Limits I've engag'd my Soul.

It is likewise necessary that he be disengag'd from Ambition, Covetousness, and all other Desires, but that of serving his Master in such an honest and moderate state of Fortune, as may preserve himself and near Relations from Envy and Necessity; for if he once begins to look after his own Advancement to Places and Honours, it cannot be otherwise, but that he will prefer his own Good to that of his Master, and serve himself first; and thus a way will be open'd to Infidelity, Perfidiousness, and Treason: There will be no Secret but he will discover, no Counsel that will not take wind, no Resolution but what he will publish, no Enemy but he will court:

Publica privatis postponed commoda rebus.

Whilst Publick Good to Private is postpon'd.

If he desire his Master's Glory, it will be only in order to advance his own; to which if he cannot arrive by serving him faithfully, he will do it by his Disservice, by selling and delivering him to his Enemies, to satisfy his Ambition or insatiable Covetousness.

> *Namq; ubi Avaritia est habitant ferme omnia ibidem*
> *Flagitia, Impietas, Perjuria, furta Rapinæ,*
> *Fraudes atque doli insidiæq; & proditiones.*
>
> Paling. In Scorp.

For all sorts of Deceits, Villanies, Thefts and Treasons reside in the same Breast with Covetousness. This is what *Stilico* practis'd heretofore, when to obtain the Friendship of *Alaric*, King of the *Goths*, and get Assistance from him to seize the *Eastern* Empire, he struck up a dishonourable Peace with him, and oblig'd the Emperor to pay him Tribute, under the Name of a Pension; and *Peter des Vignes*, Chancellor of *Frederick* the Second, had his Eyes put out, and that justly, for holding too strict and secret Correspondence with Pope *Alexander* the Third, his Master's mortal ENemy. It was for the same Reason that

Cardinal *Balue* remain'd twelve Years close Prisoner in the Tower *des Loches*, under the Reign of *Louis* the Eleventh; and that Cardinal *du Prat* was put out of Favour, and was confin'd for a long time by *Francis* the First. The same Vigor and Temper of Mind preserves our Minister from being too credulous, or superstitious, or too much a Bigot: for although *Credulitas error sit magis quam culpa, & quidem in optimi cujusq; Mentem facillime obrepat*, Clc. Book I. Ep. 23. Credulity is rather an Error than Crime, and that it most easily steals in upon the best Natures; yet it is proper for a judicious and sensible Man to believe nothing, *nisi quod in oculos incurret, (Seneca of Anger)* but what passes before his Eyes: And *Palingenius*is of Opinion, that it should be so, for fear least he should be deceiv'd, because

> *Qui facilis credit facilis quoq; fallitur idem.*

He's easily deceiv'd, who soon believes.

And as it has been laid down before, that there are four or five means to draw in and over-reach Persons too credulous and superstitious; so it is necessary, that he who would undertake to practise them, should not be so weak as to let himself be caught with them by others, that would make use of them against him. Besides, a Minister, who has a Spirit mean enough to swallow, and to submit to the Belief of so many Fables, Impostures, false Miracles, and Deceits as are generally practis'd, can give but little Hopes of his good Success in many Affairs, where all these Follies are to be pass'd over with an airy Neglect. The Condescension of Statesmen, the Artifices of Courtiers, the

Management and Practices of subtle Politicians, easily deceive a Man plung'd in excessive and superstitious Devotions. The Prediction of a Soothsayer, the Croaking of a Raven, the meeting of a Blackamore, a false Rumour, or the imaginary Approach of Danger, will make him lose his Courage, astonish him, and cause him to fall into some shameful and dishonourable Party, to which if he be never so little enclin'd by his own Nature, Superstition, the Sister of this great Credulity, shall immediately involve him, and take away that little Judgment that he has left remaining. *Occentus foricis auditus Fabio Maximo dictaturam C. Flaminio Magisterium equitum deponendi causam præbuit,* (Val. Max. *Book* I.) Upon the Hearing a Rat squeak, *Fabius Maximus* took occasion to lay down the Office of Dictator, and *Caius Flaminius* that of General of the Horse. It will rob him of the Ease of his Body, and of the Firmness, Constancy, and Resolution of his Mind. *Superstitione enim qui est imbutus quiescere nunquam potest,* says *Tully*; Superstition will subject the Party tainted with it to a thousand panick Terrors, and make him fear, *Nihilo metuenda magis quam quæ pueri in tenebris pavitant finguntq; futura*; such Phantomes, as are no more to be regarded, than those which Children frame in the dark, and then think they will approach them; it will commit more Sins than are forbidden in the Ten Commandments, and washing his Eyes with Holy Water, or touching the Cope of a Priest, he shall think that all the ill Actions of his Life shall be effac'd. *Sic errore quodam mentis famulatur impietati,* (says *Paschasius de Virtute*) By the Error of his Understanding, he becomes a Slave to Impiety. It will make him find Scruples where there are none; so that before the

Conclusion of an Affair, he shall send an hundred times for his Confessor: He will reveal to him the Counsels of his Prince, submit them to his Censure, examine them according to the Casuistical Rules, and at last *ea quæ Dei sunt audacter excludet, ut sua tantum admittat,* what he alone prescribes will be follow'd, when the Precepts of God are audaciously rejected. In short, it will render him foolish, impertinent, stupid, wicked, incapable of seeing or doing any thing, of judging or examining to any purpose, and capable only of accomplishing the Ruin of himself, and whosoever else shall make use of him. *Nam superstitione quisquis illaque atus est non potest effugere proximas miserias, ipsa sibi superstitio supplicium est, dum quæ non sunt mala hæc fingit esse talia, & quæ sunt mediocria mala hæc maxima facit ac Lethalia;* for whosoever is enslav'd with Superstition cannot avoid impending Miseries; for Superstition it self is a Punishment, whilst he imagines those things to be Mischiefs which are not so, and such Evils as are of a moderate Nature to be most extraordinary and mortal. There is no Occasion for much Mystery and Ceremony to be a good Man; *Lycurgus* was reputed such, although he retrench'd several things in the Religion of his Country, which were superfluous and unusueful. The elder *Cato* pass'd for the most virtuous of the *Romans,* although he ridicul'd the Person, who took it for an ill Augury, that the Rats had gnaw'd his Buskins, by telling him, *Non esse illud monstrum quod arrosæ sint a soricibus caligæ, sed vere monstrum habendum fuisse si sorices a caligis roderentur,* (St. Austin de Doct. Christian.) That it was no Prodigy that the Rats should gnaw the Boots, but the real Prodigy would have been, if the Boots had gnawn the Rats. *Lucullus* was not esteem'd impious, for having fought *Tigranes* upon a Day that was mark'd as unfortunate in the *Roman* Calendar; nor *Claudius* for despising those Auspices that were made by the feeding of Chickens; no more than *Lucius Æmilius Paulus*, for having been the first that demolish'd the Temples of *Serapis* and *Isis*. From whence it may easily be conjectur'd, that Superstition is the true Character of a weak, dejected, effeminate and vulgar Soul; concerning which every noble Spirit, every resolute Man and wise Minister ought to say, as *Varro* did of another thing that was not more valuable.

> *Apage in directum a domo nostro istam insanitatem.*
> In Eumennidib.

Let such Madness be directly driven from our Habitation.

The second Virtue which ought to serve for a Foundation to the Merits and Renown of our Councellor, is Justice; of which, if all the Parts were to be explain'd, it might be compar'd to a Stem, which produces three Branches, one of which rises up towards God, the second extends to ones self, and the third towards our Neighbour; and each of these Branches produces likewise several little Boughs, which I shall not particularly explain, it being sufficient here to take things in the gross. Whereupon I shall place the principal Foundation of this Justice in being an honest Man, living according to the Laws of God and Nature, nobly, philosophically, with an Integrity without Vernish, a Virtue without Art, a Religion without Fear, without Scruple, and a firm Resolution of doing good, without other Respect and Consideration, but that he ought to live so, that he may live like a Man of Honesty and Honour.

Oderunt peccare boni Virtutis amore.

The good Man hates a Crime for Virtue's Sake.

But forasmuch as this natural, universal, noble, and Philosophical Justice is sometimes out of use, and not accommodated to the Practice of the World, where *veri juris germanæq; justitiæ solidam & expressam effigiem nullam tenemus, umbris & imaginibus utimur;* We have no fix'd and express Effigies of true Law and natural Justice, but use the Shadows and Appearances of them, it will be often necessary to take up with the artificial, particular and politick one adapted and applicable to the Occasions and Necessities of Polities and States, since it is soft and pliant enough to accommodate it self as the *Lesbian* Rule to human and popular Weakness, and to divers Times, Persons, Affairs and Accidents; all which Considerations very often oblige us to several things, which natural Justice would absolutely refuse and condemn. But why, we must live as other Men, and amongst so many Corruptions, he that has the least ought to pass for the best; *Beatus qui minimus urgetur*, happy he that has the fewest. Amongst so many Vices one may sometimes legitimate one, and amongst a great many good Actions one may disguise one. So then as it is a Maxim, that amongst Lances those are the best which will bend most, so amongst Ministers they should be most esteem'd who are most compliant, and can accommodate themselves to divers Occurrences, so as to come at the End of their Designs, thereby imitating the God *Vertumnus*, who said of himself in *Propertius*;

> *Opportuna mea est cunctis natura figuris*
> *In quamcunq; voles verte decorus ero.*

> My Nature can receive what Form you will;
> But change me as you please I'm handsome still.

Let him only remember always to observe these two Precepts; the first to bring and join together Profit and Honesty, still having his Eye upon the latter, and enclining to it as much as he can possible; the second, never to serve as an Instrument of his Master's Passion, nor to propose or conclude any thing that he does not judge necessary for the Preservation of the State, the Good of the People, or the Safety of the Prince: And then as to the rest he may secure himself under the Covert of this good Advice of *Plutarch, That very often in doing Justice, there is no Necessity for all that is just.* (Book of Curiosity.)

The third and last part which should go to the Composition and Perfection of our Ministers is Prudence, a Virtue so necessary to a Man of that Quality, that he can by no means be without it, seeing, as *Aristotle* teaches us, *Prudence and Policy are the same Habits of Mind,* (Ethicks, Book 6.) and that it is so powerful that it governs us in three important Circumstances of our Lives, *it orders things present, foresees things to come, and recollects what is past:* so universal, that it comprehends under it all other Virtues, and Observations, that we can make here concerning Knowledge, Modesty, Experience, Conduct, Temper, Discretion, and particularly that which the *Italians* call *Segretezza*, by a Term proper to themselves; *Juvenal* having said (*Sat.* 10.) very justly, that *Nullum numen abest si sit Prudentia*, where-ever there is Prudence no Divinity is wanting. Nevertheless as many things are necessary for the Production of Gold, which is the King of Metals, the Preparation of the Matter, the Disposition of the Earth, the Heat of the Sun, the Length of time: so to form this Prudence, the Queen of Political Virtues, the Gold of Kingdoms, the Treasure of States, there ought to be great Assistances, and very happy Advantages; as Force of Spirit, a Soundness of Judgment, a Strength of Reason, a quick Apprehension in receiving the Instructions of great Persons, a Study of Sciences, a Knowledge of History, and a comprehensive Memory of things past, are but Dispositions towards the arriving at it; a Depth in Consultation, a Knowledge and Consideration of Circumstances, a Foresight of Effects, a Precaution against Obstacles, a speedy Dispatch are the good Actions it produces; and at last the Ease of all People, the Safety of States, the common Good of Mankind, are the Divine Fruits that will be gather'd from it. But hitherto we have said nothing, unless we add what are the Signs by which we may judge of the Progress that any one has made towards the acquiring of this Treasure, and whether he is truly wise and prudent enough to assist a Prince in the Administration of his State. Now amongst many that may be given, I shall propose these as the most usual and common, that is, to keep Secret that which is not proper to be spoke of, and to speak rather out of Necessity than Forwardness, not to believe too easily, nor all sort of Persons, to be more ready to give that which belongs to himself, than to demand that which belongs to another; to examine things thoroughly before he passes Judgment on them, to speak ill of no body, to excuse Faults, and defend every one's good Name, to despise no Person, not even the meanest, to honour Men according to their Merits and Qualities, to give the Praise to his Assistants rather than himself, to serve and gratify his Friends, remaining firm and constant to them amidst their Adversities, not to change a Design and Resolution without some urgent Reason, to deliberate with Leisure, and to execute briskly, and with Diligence: not to be struck with Admiration at that which is extraordinary, not to ridicule any Person, but especially to spare poor People and his Friends; not to deny due Praise to those who deserve it, not even to his Enemies; not to speak without Certainty, nor to give Counsel but to them that ask it; not to pretend to understand that which is not in his own Profession, nor to speak of that which it but with Modesty, and without Affectation, as *Piso* did, of whom *Velleius Paterculus* said, *Quæ agenda sunt agit sine ullâ ostentatione agendi;* to be more ready at performing than promising, to have more Patience than Violence, to desire the Good rather than the Mischief of his Enemies, rather to lose than contend, not to be the Cause of any Trouble or Disturbance; lastly to serve God, love his Neighbour, and neither to desire Death, nor to fear it. Now that which has made me so particular in collecting all these Signs, is because the choice of a Minister is of so great Importance, that Princes have an extraordinary Interest not to be deceiv'd in it; and although it is not to be hop'd, that all of them might be met with in one Man, yet he should be preferr'd that is possest of most of them. And when a Prince has found him, he is to be look'd upon and preserv'd as a precious Treasure; for though his Birth did not give him Crowns, yet they cannot easily be worn without him; though Fortune did not make him a King, his Abilities render him the Oracle of Kings, and make what he says become Laws; his single Words pass for Reasons, his Actions for Examples, and his whole Life for a Miracle.

After having explain'd what is the Duty of a Minister towards his Prince, it remains to us to consider by the way, what a Prince on his side should contribute towards the good treatment of his Minister, and because in the matter of Rules and Precepts I have always thought with *Horace*, that the shortest are the best, *Quicquid præcipies esto Brevis*, I shall reduce all those which to me seem necessary upon this occasion, to three principal ones, of which the first shall be to treat him as a Friend and not as a Servant, to speak and confer with him with an open Heart, to conceal nothing from him that he knows, but to display an entire Confidence, and treat with him as he would do with himself, without being asham'd to declare his Weakness, Ignorance, or any other failing that he may have, not even his Spite, his Hatred, Anger, Discontent, or the like Passions that may torment him. And altho' I should not have sufficient Authority to establish this Maxim, yet some deference at least may be paid to the Advice of *Seneca*, *Cogita an tibi in amicitiam aliquis recipiendus sit, quum placuerit id fieri toto illum pectore admitte, tam audacter cum illo loquere quam tecum*, Consider well whether a Person is fit to be receiv'd into your Friendship; but when you are pleas'd so to do, admit him entirely to your Breast, and speak as boldly and freely with him as you would to your self. It is that which he had said before, but in fewer Words, *Tu omnia cum amico delibera sed de eo prius*, deliberate with your Friend concerning all things, but first deliberate concerning him. But if so great a Man's Authority must be supported and maintained by some Reasons, *Titus Livius* will furnish us with one that is very valuable and prevalent; *Vult sibi quisque credi, & habita fides ipsam fidem obligat*, every one would be confided in, and Confidence once plac'd obliges to Confidence. Experienc'd Chymists say, that nothing is to be us'd towards the making of Gold but Gold it self.

> *Neve aliunde petas Auri primordia, in Auro*
> *Semina sunt auri, quamvis abstrusa recedant*
> *Longius, & multo nobis quærenda labore.*
> Augurellus.

> Seek not elsewhere for Gold's Original,
> The Seeds of Gold remain in Gold it self;
> Although abstruse, far off in dark Recess,
> There to be sought with Art and wondrous Pains.

The Lapidaries shew us every Day, that one Diamond must be used to cut another; the Bird-Catchers, to succeed in their Sport, make use of Decoy Birds, which *Varro* calls *Illices & Traditores generis sui*, The moral Philosophers say,

177

that Love cannot be obtain'd but by a mutual Affection and Friendship. How then can a Prince find Confidence in any Friend, if he be not first communicative on his own part, if he does not first shew him his Duty by acquitting himself of his own, *Si vis me flere dolendum est, primum ipsi tibi*, you must first weep your self, if you would have me shed Tears, said *Horace. Et cur te habebo ut Consulem si non me habeas ut Senatorem?* Why should I esteem you as a Consul, if you will not look upon me as a Senator, reply'd another? All must be done or nothing, and an entire Confidence must be plac'd or none at all: To declare a thing one Day, and to conceal another to Morrow, to begin a thing, and not to go thorough with it, to keep something always as a *Retentum* upon the *Reserve*, and not to say all, are marks of Distrust, Uneasiness, and Irresolution, which makes a Minister lose the Prospect he should have in his Councils, and that Affection which should make him concern'd for his Service.

The second thing a Man should observe towards his Minister, is that he hold him for a Friend, and not as a Flatterer; that he permit him to speak, and give his Opinion freely, and to explain and support it, without constraining, or showing any Resentment for not condescending to his. *Meliora enim vulnera diligentis quam oscula blandientis*, for the Wounds of a Friend are better than the Kisses of a Flatterer; seeing as a bold Counsellor told his Master, *Non potes me simul amico & adulatore uti*, I cannot be a Friend, if you will make use of me as a Flatterer. If a Prince will be flatter'd, there are Courtiers enough who only wait for an Occasion of doing it, without employing him in that matter, whose Mouth ought to be his Oracle of Truth. And that

Person can never succeed well, *cujust aures ita formatæ sunt ut aspera quæ utilia & nihil nisi jucundum non læsurum accipiant,* (says *Tacitus*) whose Ears are so form'd that such things sound harsh as are useful, and can hear nothing but what is pleasant, and sure not to offend them.

Lastly, as they who stay sometime in the Sun-shine are warm'd b the Heat of it; so it is fitting, that he who is suffer'd by a Prince or Sovereign to approach his Person, should feel the Effects of his Power, and the Friendship he bears him, as a Recompence due to his Services; and although the most honourable and glorious that he can give him is that of declaring himself satisfied, and that they are agreeable to him, yet he ought to go farther, and upon this Occasion to practise the generous Virtue of Liberality, by supplying him with things necessary for his living in a moderate and decent Port, and as far from Want as Ambition. *Philip* the Second said to *Ruy Gomez* his Servant and Confident, *Do you look after my Affairs, and I'll provide for yours.* All Princes should say as much to their Ministers, if they would be serv'd with Faithfulness and Affection. *Liberalitas enim commune quoddam vinculum est, quo beneficus & beneficio devinctus astringuuntur;* for Liberality is a sort of common TIe, with which he that does the good Office, and he that receives it, are mutually bound to one another. And it is my Thought, that it is best to set them at Ease in that matter, that so having no Apprehension of that horrible Monster *Poverty,* they may bring a Mind entirely free and disingag'd from all Passions to the Management of Affairs, which will be the first Recompence of this Liberality, whereas the Second will be the Honour of him that practices it; for, according to *Aristotle, Amongst all Princes inclin'd to Virtue, they are the most belov'd, who have the Fame and Reputation of being liberal.* The last will be the rendring those Persons entirely devoted to their Service; seeing according to the Saying of an Ancient, *He that first invented Benefits was the first that made Trails, and found out Casting-Nets to make Men Captives, and draw them after him.*

So, my Lord, this is all that I have remaining to say of this matter, which I had never undertaken to treat of, unless in Obedience to the Commands of your Eminency; and if your great Condescension and Goodness did not make me hope for a favourable Excuse for the Faults that I may have committed: I know that it requir'd greater Parts than mine, a Pen more fluent, a Learning more accomplish'd, a stronger Judgment, and a Genius more universal; but we should have had few Statues of *Jupiter*, if no Person had been permitted to carve them but *Phidias*; and *Rome* would be very empty of Paintings, if no other Person had been suffer'd to draw but *Michael Angelo* and *Raphael Urbin*. Good Workmen are not so often to be found, but that indifferent ones may be employ'd; nor such great Politicians, but sometimes one may be entertain'd with the Works of the less: Under which Title if your Eminency shall please to shelter this present Discourse, it will oblige me to think of undertaking something greater; and I dare promise my self, under the Continuation of your Favour and Patronage,

Illa dies olim veniet (modo stamina vitæ

Longa trahat Lechesis) quumte & tua facta cananius
Uberius, nomenq; tuum Gangetica tellus,
Et Tartessiaci resonabunt littora ponti.
Ibit Hyper boreas passim tua fama per urbes,
Et per me extremis Libyæ nosceris in oris,
Tunc ego majori Musarum percitus œstro,
Omnibus ostendam quanto tenearis amore
Justitiæ, sit quanta tibi Pietasq; Fidesq;
Quantum consilio valeas & fortibus ausis,
Quam fis munificus, quam clemens, denique per me,
Ingenium moresq; tuos mirabitur orbis;
At nunc ista tibi quæ tradimus accipe læto
Interea vultu & præsentibus annue cœptis.

These Verses, with some small Paraphrase, may be very properly apply'd to the most Noble Person, upon whom the Success of this Translation must entirely depend.

The time will come, (if Fate shall please to give,
This feeble Thread of mine more space to live)
When I shall you, and all your Acts rehearse,
In a much loftier and more fluent Verse,
To Ganges *Banks, and* China *farther East,*
To Carolina, *and the distant West,*
Your Name shall fly, and ev'ry where be blest;
Through Spain *and Tracts of* Lybian *Sands shall go*
To Russian *Limits, and to* Zembla's *Snow*
Then shall my eager Muse expand her Wing,
Your Love of Justice, and your Goodness sing,
Your Greatness equal to the State you hold,
In Counsel wise, in Execution bold;

How there appears in all that you dispense
Bounty, Good-nature, and the Strength of Sense;
These let the World admire! □ From you a Smile,
Is more than a Reward for all my Toil.

FINIS.